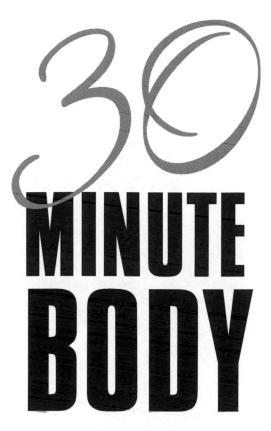

30 MINUTE BODY

World Champion
Personal Training
Secrets Revealed!

LANCE McCULLOUGH

Publisher's Cataloging-In-Publication Data
(Prepared by The Donohue Group, Inc.)

Names: McCullough, Lance. | Simeonov, Daniel, illustrator.
Title: 30 minute body : world champion personal training secrets revealed! /
    Lance McCullough ; illustrations by Daniel Simeonov.
Other Titles: Thirty minute body
Description: Upland, CA : Fitness Results, [2016] | Includes bibliographical references.
Identifiers: ISBN 978-0-692-79189-9 | ISBN 978-1-5323-2576-2 (ebook)
Subjects: LCSH: Physical fitness. | Isometric exercise. | Weight training. | Aerobic
    exercises. | Nutrition. | Weight loss.
Classification: LCC GV481 .M33 2016 (print) | LCC GV481 (ebook) |
    DDC 613.7--dc23

Published by Fitness Results
1842 W. 11th St. #G
Upland, CA 91786
(909) 608-1780

E-mail:info@fitnessresults.com
Web: www.30minutebody.com
Web: www.fitnessresults.com
Web: www.fitnessresultstrainingsystem.com

Printed in the United States
Illustrations by Daniel Simeonov

*To my wife Susie for her constant support
while I pursue my fitness dreams.*

Table of Contents

CHAPTER 1

About The 30-Minute Body Book

Here's a startling fact – only three 30-minute workouts a week, when coupled with a well-balanced diet based on natural foods, is enough resistant weight bearing exercise for you to lose weight, achieve a toned, healthy body, increase your strength, flexibility and balance, promote mental health and overall well-being.

This book will provide the information you need to help you determine your health and fitness destination. It will cover all the topics that affect the journey so you arrive at your destination safely, efficiently and effectively. By using the information in this book, you will stay on the road to your destination without getting lost or heading in the wrong direction. I'll steer you away from road hazards and congested traffic while shortening your travel time.

In this book I share stories of the journeys of past clients, showing you what they did to stay on the road and how they got back on the right road after getting lost. For some clients, the journey is long and I had to keep nudging them back to the road. Some clients settled for a destination that was nearer. Some even gave up. Some clients required motivation to get started; others initially thought they lacked the potential to start toward the destination.

I haven't held anything back. This book reveals all my personal training secrets. They are based on common sense training methods that you don't usually hear about, or are presented in a confusing or unclear manner. My goal is to teach you all my secrets in clear language that makes sense. So let's get started!

Secret #1: The health and fitness industry has been lying to you!

The health and fitness industry has been leading you down a dangerous road to an unclear destination that is not very attractive. What this means is that the industry has been lying to you!

Instead of using common sense to test whether a newly-announced trend is safe, effective and efficient, health and fitness professionals jump on the bandwagon and push the newest fad. They don't take the time to weigh the risks versus the rewards, or evaluate the benefits versus the time investment. Perhaps these professionals lack confidence or knowledge, so take the path of least resistance. Or maybe they are influenced by so-called leaders in the industry and are afraid of becoming unpopular if they don't follow the leader.

I'm a fitness professional who is not afraid to stand up for what is right even if it is not popular. I'm not afraid to call out a bad practice, especially if it will save my clients time, money and stress while helping them achieve their health and fitness goals.

Here's an example of what I'm talking about. Core training – situps, crunches, reverse crunches, side crunches, hanging leg raises, etc. – is frequently recommended as a fitness program. It consistently appears in the annual fitness trend forecast published by the American College of Sports Medicine (ACSM). The forecast is based on survey responses from thousands of fitness professionals, and lists the Top 20 trends for each year.

Between 2007 and 2010, core training was listed at #5. Between 2011 and 2015, it bounced around at #6, #7, #9, #13 and #15 respectively. In 2016, it slipped to #19 out of 20 trends – just barely making the list.

How could this happen? If core training is essential, how could it move so dramatically over a nine-year period? The answer is simple. New trends appeared and pushed core training aside. Body weight training, high intensity interval training (HIIT), and now even wearables (the #1 trend in the 2016 ACSM survey) have overtaken core training. And as core training has slipped in popularity, information is coming out about the hidden dangers of area-specific training.

Interestingly, strength training, which is what I recommend in the 30-Minute Body book, has consistently been in the Top 5.

A new exercise gaining popularity is the plank. There are many plank techniques, but I want to discuss the one that is basically a pushup position at full arm extension. The goal is to hold that position as long as you can, and to increase the time with every repetition. 30 seconds is good; one minute is even better.

Doing the plank or walking the plank are both risky.

I see all kinds of articles touting the benefits of the plank. What I don't see is information on the negatives. The stated benefit of the plank is strengthening the core. But muscle strength is built by movement. The plank is an isometric exercise, and therefore produces minimal muscle development and very little increased strength. It does produce soreness which gives the illusion of benefit. But the plank requires investing a lot of time to produce minimum results. Although isometric exercises are slightly better than nothing and can be used in physical therapy when nothing else is available, it is not an efficient way to strengthen core muscles.

The plank comes with a lot of negatives. When in the plank position, you are holding up your entire body weight for extended periods. This puts a lot of stress on your wrists, elbows and shoulders. If you weigh 150 lbs. and I asked you to lay on the bench press and hold a bar weighing 75 lbs. for 30 seconds to one minute, you would say, *no way,* especially if your bench press was less than that. But that's exactly what you'd be doing with the plank.

Doing the plank puts your wrists, elbows and shoulders at risk of injury, creates discomfort, and results in minimal core strengthening. Common sense should tell you that the risks outweigh the benefits and that there must be a better way to achieve a stronger core. (Hint: there is!)

Let's analyze another popular body weight exercise – the burpee. To perform a burpee, you begin in a standing position, go to a squatting forward position with hands on the ground, kick your feet out to a pushup position, return to squatting position and back to standing position, then repeat. Depending on your body weight, you could be putting 600+ lbs. of pressure on your upper body with each rep when you consider the relationship between distance, time, velocity, speed and impact force.

Imagine that you have a piece of wood that you want to drive a nail into. If you take a 24 oz. hammer and set it gently on top of a nail, the nail will fall over when you remove the hammer. However, if you raise the hammer away from the nail then drop the hammer head, you will drive the nail into the wood. Raise the hammer higher and bring it down with greater force, and you'll drive the nail even further into the wood.

The burpee movement is like using a hammer (your body weight) to drive a nail. The faster and more vigorously you do the exercise, the more force you put on your body and the greater the risk of injury. Unless you are an athlete looking for peak performance, the risk will never outweigh the rewards.

Exercises like the plank and burpee are being touted as what you must do to start an exercise program. No wonder people are apprehensive about starting a health and fitness program. The health and fitness industry adopts exercises meant for elite athletes, then tells beginners that this is what they have to do. ***This is absolutely not what you should be doing.*** I am 53 years old and a champion weight lifter, and this is not appealing to me at all. I am in exceptional shape without using risky exercises, and can assure you that you do not have to do planks, burpees and similar exercises to achieve your health and fitness goals.

Americans are spending more on health and fitness yet are in the worst state of overall health and fitness ever. The health and fitness industry caters to those who are looking for an instant and easy way to achieve their health and fitness goals by developing "miracle" products and programs. Self-proclaimed experts make promising claims and pay for celebrity endorsements. The media publicizes the product or program and people flock to them because they are desperate and hope that this time, it will be different.

My guarantee to you: this time it *will* be different!

Now is the time to personally take charge of your own health and fitness by using the knowledge in this book. I am so confident that my methods work that I give you this guarantee: if you don't think this book added value or resulted in positive changes to your overall health and fitness, I will refund your money, no questions asked. You're on the honor system. Just send me your purchase receipt and contact information and you'll receive my check for a full refund. To help me learn from your experience, I'd appreciate your sharing why my program didn't work for you.

Benefits of Resistance Weight Training

I often claim that resistance weight training and exercise is the closest thing you'll ever find to a fountain of youth. It benefits both body and mind; muscles, bones and brain; and contributes to your quality of life by keeping you strong and active. While all this might sound too good to be true, it's not.

Before I discuss the benefits of resistance weight training, I must state a caveat: *you will only realize the full benefit if you follow the guidelines given in the 30-Minute Body*. Sadly, most people working out aren't doing that. I estimate that as few as 7-8% of all people who exercise regularly at home or in a gym are actually achieving all the possible benefits.

Resistance weight training benefits your entire body, but especially your muscles, bones, joints, heart, skin, metabolism and brain. It has a positive effect on your strength, stamina, balance, coordination, flexibility, body shape, energy level and outlook on life.

Muscles and Bones

A resistance weight training program will cause you to gain or increase your muscle mass. This makes you stronger and gives you the ability to do more things with greater ease. Your muscles become better defined, adding contours to your body that produce a desirable and appealing shape. Women who build muscle mass acquire a more feminine shape, while men look more masculine.

You'll be building stronger bones, making them less porous and slowing down the rate of bone loss that occurs normally as you age.

Joint Stability

Stronger muscles and bones mean more joint stability, protecting your body from injury like a suit of armor. You'll be less prone to arthritis and premature wearing of the joints. As you lose weight, you will reduce the stress on joints like knees and ankles. By building a better balanced musculoskeletal system, your entire body will function harmoniously, further reducing the risk of injury, aches and pains.

Higher Resting Metabolic Rate

As muscle mass builds, you need more calories to sustain your weight at rest, resulting in a higher resting metabolic rate. A resistance weight training workout raises your metabolic rate for up to 23 hours as your body deals with cellular disorientation, the result of lifting and pushing with maximum effort. Your cells get out of sequence, requiring extra energy to re-sequence. The resequencing process can take up to 23 hours, and your metabolic rate will continue to be slightly elevated for an additional 12 hours.

Brain Function

As you work your muscles, you increase blood flow to the brain. It takes a lot of brain activity to coordinate the mechanisms of the body, and increased blood flow helps the brain make everything work together. I fully expect that future scientific discoveries will show even greater benefits to the brain from resistance weight training than we know of today, including reducing the risk of Alzheimer's disease.

Coordination

Resistance weight training promotes greater coordination by increasing the mind-muscle connection, training muscle fibers to work together more effectively, increasing your body awareness, and enhancing brain function.

With the increased strength, cardiovascular conditioning, blood flow and cell rejuvenation that results from resistance weight training, your entire body will function better. You will have more energy, feel more active and productive, and perform daily tasks better.

Cardiovascular Condition and Health

Resistance weight training can contribute to VO2 Max (maximal oxygen uptake) which is related to recovery heart rate (how fast your heart recovers and returns to a lower rate after being elevated). This is an important measure of good health and promotes lower blood pressure.

Skin

A recent study of people over 60 years old who exercise regularly found that their skin was similar to that of 30-40 year olds. A group of 65-year-olds who had not been exercising began 30-minute workouts twice a week. After three months, the group had skin comparable to 30-40 year olds. While exercise does not reverse skin damage due to sun exposure, it does reverse damage from the aging process.

Outlook on Life

When you are healthy, strong, and at the right weight, your outlook on life will improve. You'll be less prone to depression, will feel motivated and able to make healthy choices, have confidence and self-esteem. You will reduce your risk of illness and sleep better.

All this sounds too good to be true, but it's not. It is the reason why I claim that resistance weight training is the closest thing there is to the fountain of youth.

Secret #2: I know what I'm talking about.

I am a world champion bench press lifter and I have conducted over 100,000 personal training sessions as a certified personal trainer. From my competition days, I learned what kind of training regimen worked for me – and for my competitors. As a personal trainer, I have learned what works for all different kinds of people – youth and seniors; professional and amateur athletes; Baby Boomers, Gen Xers, Millennials. I learned and applied the science of training on my road to becoming a world champion. I perfected the art of training in more than 100,000 personal training sessions with clients.

I have combined the science and art of training into my unique health and fitness program that is safe, efficient and effective.

As a gym owner, I have hired many personal trainers over the years. From this I have learned that bodybuilders and weightlifters know the art but not the science of training. These trainers might suggest that a client undertake a training regimen that was not the best or the safest – because the trainer only knew what worked for their training, but lacked knowledge of the science. These trainers did not know how to balance the risk versus the reward of a client's training program. That inevitably led to compromising safety, efficiency and effectiveness, producing less-than-desirable fitness results.

Likewise, a trainer with a college degree – maybe even an advanced degree, or a degree in physical therapy – may understand the science but not the art. While safety might not be an issue, efficiency and effectiveness are because these trainers lack basic knowledge of the gym environment. Again, that leads to a compromise on efficiency and effectiveness of the training regime.

My success as a personal trainer is based on my knowledge of the science of health and fitness – the mechanics of how to achieve goals – and the art of training – learning how to successfully guide a client to achieving his or her goals. What I add to this is the ability to educate clients with easy-to-understand instructions and explanations. That's the heart of this book – my realization that achieving fitness results is all about choices. If you are given the right information that is easy to understand, you gain knowledge and become empowered to make the right choices.

Personal training clients at my gym are given information that keeps them engaged and interested in the training process. They are not blind followers of instructions and are not looking for the quick fix. Instead, they want to know what lies behind the training methods and the nutrition program. They want to understand why the trainers do this instead of that. They are curious about why the trainers appear to contradict conventional information about personal training or nutrition.

This book is the next-best thing to being a personal training client at my gym, Fitness Results. In it I've revealed my secrets, knowing it will inspire you to realize your fitness goals. I'll give you information to help you through the tough times. I'll prepare you to make the most of your workout time and to take control of your fitness goals when outside the gym.

This book is a compilation of textbook learning and practical application gathered over more than 20 years in the fitness industry. Like all such compilations, it won't answer every question or fit every individual circumstance. While hundreds of clients have benefited from and achieved their fitness goals using the methods discussed in this book, it won't work for everyone, every time, in every circumstance. So when you are reading the book, use common sense and strive to understand the spirit of the words as well as their exact meaning. And if you have a specific medical or physical condition for which you have received advice that is at odds with what is in this book, follow the advice of your medical professional.

Now let's get to work on **Your Fitness Results.**

Why You Can Trust Me

I've had a passion for health and fitness training since high school. My initial interest in resistance weight training was to enhance my performance potential on the football team, but I soon discovered that weightlifting was my true passion.

While still in high school, I joined a gym where I combined my natural ability with hard work and a personal training regimen. That led me to competing nationally and internationally as a weight lifter. In 1998 my competition career reached its highest point when I won the Amateur Athletic Union World Bench Press Championship and set a new world record.

Always a motivated self-starter, I have a lifelong pattern of challenging myself and pushing my limits. During high school I earned the rank of Eagle Scout. With the support of my parents, I worked during high school and at age 18 was the youngest person ever to enter the meat cutter apprentice program from the grocery chain that employed me. I paid my own way through the program, learning a lot about business in the process.

During my years in competition, I developed my personal philosophy of how to use resistance weight training to achieve health and fitness goals. I have been applying my philosophy ever since to benefit my personal fitness clients. Certified as a personal trainer by the Aerobics and

LEFT: My trophy for winning the 1998 AAU World Bench Press championship. **RIGHT:** Coming off stage after receiving my two trophies for the Open 275 and Submaster over age 35 categories.

Fitness Association of America (AFAA) since 1989, I have been working in the fitness industry for over 30 years.

After managing several gyms on behalf of others, my wife Susie and I opened Fitness Results in 1994. In addition to my personal training clientele, I employ other personal trainers who have completed the Fitness Results internship program run in conjunction with a local community college. I speak to groups on topics related to health and fitness. I also serve as a consultant to private businesses wishing to develop fitness programs for their employees. In these instances, I've designed a gym at the business location, procured the equipment, and hired personal training staff that helps employees become and stay fit and healthy. And fit, healthy employees mean an improved bottom line for the business.

Besides activities within the fitness industry, I support many community organizations. I refurbished a local high school weight training room with up-to-date and safe equipment; donated equipment to the YMCA and other organizations; and regularly donate to health- and fitness-related causes. I recently organized an effort to send care packages to troops overseas.

My personal mission is to change society's views on the importance of resistance weight training and proper nutrition as the basis of a health and fitness program that improves coordination, promotes healthy bones and muscles, and acts to reduce the effects of disease, and aging.

CHAPTER *2*

My Training Philosophy

Congratulations on making the decision to improve your health and well-being. Whether your motivation is to lose weight, improve your fitness level, become healthier, or something else, I will help you acquire the knowledge it takes to be successful. This training book will guide you into a quality fitness program — one that is simple and based on choices you make that fit your life.

Your health and fitness is a journey. Like any journey, it is important to have directions and find the way that works best for you to get to your destination.

- *Some people prefer the shortest, fastest and safest route.* This is what I recommend. It just makes sense, and is the basis for this book.
- *Some like a scenic route.* I don't like this route, as it isn't efficient. Why waste your time and effort to receive only minimum benefits?
- *Some prefer the most challenging route.* Personally, I don't believe

anyone who is knowledgeable and has been given good advice would pick this route. It is dangerous and may produce injury instead of health and fitness.

A Client Dialog about Alternatives to Resistance Weight Training

Colleen sent me a Facebook video of women in a swimming pool doing a water aerobics pole dance routine. She thought it looked like a fun alternative to resistance weight training. If you're not familiar with pole dancing, it is a dance using a pole as an apparatus to support the body while performing movements on it and against it. I've been told that pole dancing was perfected in strip clubs. I first saw it at an IHRSA (International Health, Racquet & Sportsclub Association) trade show as a new fitness idea that people would like. The women doing the demo were in great shape, very fit and clearly had developed a lot of skill using the pole. They could do all kinds of move on that pole . . . wow! Wait – I lost my train of thought – what was I talking about? Oh, yes, water aerobics pole dancing in the video – a very innovative exercise technique.

Here's my exchange with Colleen, including a comment by David, one of Colleen's Facebook friends, who holds a doctorate in physical therapy.

Here's my take on the idea of making fun the most important criteria for selecting an exercise program. While initially you may be more motivated to exercise because it is fun, you'll probably find that it takes a lot more "fun" to achieve fitness results than to knuckle down and do three 30-minute weight training sessions a week. Just because an activity is fun, and therefore engaging, doesn't mean it is helping you meet your health and fitness goals.

While it is true that something is better than nothing, let's dig a little deeper. Stopping your education in eighth grade is better than having no education at all. But continuing your education for four more years, through high school, will put you ahead in the long run. You'll spend more time and energy throughout your entire life, just to make up what would have been your high school years. So why would you settle for the equivalent of an eighth grade education in health and fitness when continuing on ultimately will produce better results for the effort expended?

Become educated and make your own decision based on common sense and what is the best choice for you. For some people, something is better than nothing. But for people who want to make positive changes to their health and fitness, a commitment to learning what you need to know to make good decisions is the best and fastest way to realize success. Fun is fun; it is not a path to fitness results. Do what is needed first and what is fun second.

Secret #3: The right exercise program takes less time and is more beneficial than you think.

Don't be a blind follower of fitness fads. Do your own research from knowledgeable sources to find the best health and fitness program for you to achieve your health and fitness goals. For people with a low tolerance for working out who don't want to push past their comfort level, then something is better than nothing. Example: a new client told me on her first appointment that she never wanted to lift more than the 15 lb. dumbbells. So she never did. But she did train with me for several years and was able to make considerable health and fitness improvements despite her set limitations. This is a good example of *something is better than nothing*.

You're familiar with the saying *no pain, no gain.* In the next story, the saying could have been *no gain, all or too much pain.* One day Natalie stopped by the gym to ask for help. She had been working out at a popular chain gym whose training method is based around Olympic weightlifting. She had been working out 5-6 days a week for more than an hour a day for several months. Natalie explained she was always tired and her body ached all the time. On top of that, she was not losing any weight and wasn't happy with the way she looked. She asked, "Can you help me?"

I told Natalie I could promise her great results in only three 30-minute sessions a week. Naturally she was skeptical, but as I explained my training method and why it works so well, she became convinced and couldn't wait to get started. Natalie was so excited that she explained her plans to her husband David over dinner. She called me the next day to ask if David could join her in the workout. She said that in all the years they'd been married and she has been going to the gym, he never wanted to go with her. But after hearing about my training philosophy, he became very excited to work out with her.

I got them started together and right away they both started seeing results. Natalie began feeling better immediately – no more aches and pains and much more energy. Best of all, she started losing weight and lots of inches. These great results required less than a quarter of the weekly time investment she had been making. Natalie and David rekindled a bond of something they could enjoy together. Based on their success, they encouraged their daughter Paige, who was participating in Olympic weightlifting competitions, to join and she began seeing great improvements, too.

Natalie: 50 years old, 5'7"

6-month comparison

	Beginning training	After 6 months	Change
Weight	170 lbs.	155 lbs.	↓15 lbs.
Body fat percentage	35%	30%	↓5%
Fat lbs.	60 lbs.	50 lbs.	↓10 lbs.
Chest	40"	37.5"	↓2.5"

	Beginning training	After 6 months	Change
Waist	35"	33"	↓2"
Hips	44.5"	41.5"	↓3"
Upper leg	26.5"	24.5"	↓2"
Middle leg	22.5"	20"	↓2.5"
Arm	13"	11.5"	↓1.5"

Natalie doing shoulder press. I'm spotting; husband David and daughter Paige are watching.

I have a lot of emotion when I relate the story of Natalie and David. About two years after starting their training with me, David was diagnosed with an aggressive form of lung cancer. He passed away less than twelve months after the diagnosis. I am thankful they were able to have the time in the gym that brought them closer together as a couple and as a family, and that I was able to contribute to it. I continue to train Natalie and her daughter. R.I.P. David – we miss you at the gym.

Secret #4: Working out is as good for the mind and spirit as it is for the body.

Imagine you are on a journey that includes a river with rushing rapids, alligators and piranhas, and a bridge to cross the river right on the path.

Those who like a fast and safe route will take the bridge across the river. Those who like a scenic route may travel down the river, do some sightseeing, hope to find another way to cross the river, and eventually make their way back to the bridge. The thrill seekers may try to cross the river without the bridge, just to say they did it.

Picking the right fitness program is similar to making that journey. During your training sessions, we will provide information that shows you how to use the bridge and avoid the dangerous route that often results in discomfort, pain and even injury. **In fitness training, *more* is not always better. The *quality* of your fitness program is much more important to achieving results than the quantity.**

Here are some goals our clients have for fitness training: lose weight and look fit; feel more comfortable in clothes; stop taking a medication; lower BMI or body fat percentage; be able to play sports; compete in a fitness contest. Your training regimen works best when it is aimed at your goals, so set aside all you have heard or read about fitness and training programs and apply yourself to learning the combination of weight and cardio training, nutrition and mental attitude that will ensure your success.

We're working together to achieve your Fitness Results.

Fitness is Mind and Body

We can say this with confidence: when you add an exercise program to your daily routine, you will be motivated to achieve your health and fitness goals. You'll eat better, you'll sleep better and be more productive, and you'll create time for slower-paced activities like walking the dog and going for a bike ride. You'll have a new positive, confident attitude. Combine this with determination, persistence, focus, patience and realistic goals and you'll achieve success.

Your mental attitude plays an important role in achieving your health and fitness goals. It is the confidence to move up to the next weight or get the extra rep while keeping good form. It is sticking to your nutrition plan no matter what happens during the day. It is finding the positives instead of the negatives in all situations. For example, if you don't achieve the new single rep maximum you were trying for, don't see it as a failure. View it as motivation to continue your workout program knowing that soon you will conquer that weight and will be moving on to the next weight. One day you'll realize that you're regularly doing things that you never thought you could.

Secret #5: Inhibitions can sabotage your success.

Inhibitions, also known as mental blocks, can sabotage your success. Even I had to learn how to conquer my mental fears. I was just 15 years old when I joined a gym for the first time. I was excited to finally have access to an unlimited amount of weight. I wanted to challenge myself and see what I really could do. I was doing curls with the EZ curl bar. After completing a set, I would add more weight. After a few sets, I was up to 170 lbs. – a pretty big weight. I remember some of the older members commenting, "Why are you doing so much weight? Are you trying to show off?" That made me think I wasn't supposed to lift that much weight. So I lightened the weight and stopped heavy lifting, keeping the weight at what I noticed the other members were lifting.

Even though I had cut back, I was still lifting more than some of the older members, who continued to make disparaging comments. A man I had seen in the gym came up to me and told me not to listen to the naysayers. He said they were jealous and wished they could lift like me. From that time on I have never cared about what others thought. I always do the best I could for me. The man who gave me the advice is a bodybuilder named Lou who had won the Junior USA bodybuilding championship several times. He could have turned professional but never wanted to. He became a good friend and mentor and was fond of telling people about this young kid that could lift huge amounts of weight.

This story has another side. My cousin Lisa joined a gym but was embarrassed to go back because she thought she was not strong enough.

She called me to see if I would train her. I found that she truly wasn't that strong, but not because she wasn't able. She had never worked out with weights before and was using 2.5 – 5 lbs., much less than other women. She was making improvements, but so slowly she thought she should stop trying. I told her she was strong enough and what she was lifting now didn't matter, that she would improve with training.

After training with me for several months and gaining strength, Lisa was scheduled to go on vacation meaning she'd miss a week of working out. I gave her a workout to do while she was gone. When I saw her after she returned from vacation, she told me she was lifting more than any other woman. Now suddenly she was so strong that other women made negative comments. I told her my story and said not to worry about what other people think or say. She continued to work out and achieved great health and fitness results.

Lisa: 36 years old, 5'6"

14-month comparison

	Beginning training	After 14 months	Change
Weight	175 lbs.	138 lbs.	↓37 lbs.
Body fat percentage	34.5%	22.5%	↓12%
Fat lbs.	60 lbs.	31 lbs.	↓29 lbs.
Chest	41"	35"	↓6"
Waist	35.5"	27"	↓8.5"
Hips	46"	38.75"	↓7.25"
Upper leg	27.5"	23"	↓4.5"
Middle leg	21.5"	18.75"	↓2.75"
Arm	13"	11.5"	↓1.5"

Ladies: don't limit yourself to conformity by using too little weight. Guys: don't compete and lift more than you can safely and with proper form. Don't compare yourself to others. Do your best and don't worry about what other people think.

Secret #6: Your own mind can sabotage your success

At the age of 19, I struggled with my squats. I was stuck at a 405 lb. squat for one rep. It was frustrating and didn't make sense. I could leg press with all the weights the machine had for lots of reps; leg curl the stack easily for lots of reps and sets; and the same with the leg extension. My bench press was close to 500 lbs. at the time, so why couldn't I increase my squat weight every time I did the exercise? I thought I was giving it my all, I really wanted to improve, and I was willing to work hard. So why wasn't I improving my results?

One day at the gym a group of other power lifters were doing squats while I was doing my squats at another machine. A guy named Larry Kidney, a world record lifter at the time, was there and regularly doing well over 880 lbs. I remember Larry had six 45-lb. weights on the bar – that's 585 lbs., well under what he would do regularly. He got set under the bar, took it off the rack, stepped back, got set to start, squatted down, then dumped the weight on the ground.

Everyone asked if Larry was okay – he said he was fine but he just didn't have it today. I remember thinking that even the greatest lifters sometime have off days, and it's okay to fail if that happens. Larry stripped the bar down to 455 lbs. (four 45-lb. plates + one 25-lb. plate + the bar. An aside: when talking about how many plates you use, you only count one side. So if I said I bench pressed four plates, that's 405 lbs. – eight plates x 45 lbs. each + the bar at 45 lbs.)

Larry turned to me and said, "Lance, you're up now." Remember, my best squat was barely 405 lbs. I replied, "Larry, you know I don't squat with you guys." Larry responded, "Who says you don't?" With that, I thought, "Why not – I have nothing to lose." Larry spotted me. I got under the bar, got set, and all the guys were cheering me on. I did the first squat and remember thinking that it felt light. I think I did six reps. I realized then that my subconscious fear of failing was causing me to fail. In that moment, I overcame my fear of failing and later became a world class squatter.

I use my own life experiences to help my clients overcome their mental blocks. Take the case of Soumaya. She wanted to transition from modeling to fitness modeling. She had never trained with weights but was dedicated to doing whatever it took to make the change. I started training her five days a week and she was making good progress. Suddenly she stopped gaining in key areas, including the incline dumbbell press. She could do three sets of 15+ reps at 20 lbs. but could not do one rep with the 25 lb. dumbbell.

This did not make sense to me. I guessed she had a mental block, so I devised a test. Before her next chest workout, I switched the end caps (the metal plate that holds the weight on the bar and also has a sticker that shows the weight) of the 20-lb. and 25-lb.weights. I put the weights back in the weight rack according to what was on the end cap, essentially switching the 20- and 25-lb. weights. When Soumaya began her incline dumbbell press workout, she did a warmup. Then I told her to start with the 20 lb. dumbbell, secretly knowing it was the 25-lb. Remember, she had never before been able to do even one rep at 25 lbs. This time did 15 reps as usual, thinking it was the 20-lb. weight. I didn't say a word. She took a rest and I told her to try the 25-lb. dumbbell (actually, the 20-lb. weight). She said, "I can't do 25 lbs." I said, "Let's try it – see if you can do one today." She grabbed the dumbbell marked 25 lbs. (really the 20-lb. weight), got set, brought the weights to her chest to start the press, and pressed with what looked like everything she's got. The dumbbells didn't budge. She gave up, racked the dumbbells and said, "I told you I can't do 25 lbs." I said, "Well, you already did 25 lbs. for 15 reps" but she didn't believe me. When I told her what I had done and verified the weights on the scale, she knew she had conquered her mental block. She went on to become a fitness model and fitness competitor.

Secret #7: Resistance weight training and exercise are the closest things to the fountain of youth and will keep your body, mind and spirit youthful.

Studies show that resistance weight training increases brain function in people over 60 years old and that regular exercise reduces the risk of

Alzheimer's disease. But don't mistake physical or mental exertion for a workout. A real workout is a period of physical exercise that you do in order to improve your fitness, ability or performance.

Secret #8: 150 minutes of moderate exercise a week can greatly reduce your risk of Alzheimer's disease! And start now - related brain changes can begin 20 years before you show symptoms of Alzheimer's disease.

A thrill seeker who takes on a challenge for its own sake is misguided. Improvement will be minimal and the likelihood of an injury is high. A sightseer who picks an exercise because others are doing it or it is the latest fad has failed to align the exercise with goals. Without the proper program and form, the fitness results cannot be achieved. The person who achieves their health and fitness goals is the one who takes the time to get good directions, who follows the safest and most direct route, is guided by common sense and good choices, and stays on a consistent course.

Weight training exercises + proper form, intensity and duration +
mental attitude = Fitness Results

Attitude and Your Fitness Results

Your mental attitude has a direct bearing on achieving your Fitness Results. Here are some tips to apply as you work toward your health and fitness goals.

- **Be positive.** You have the right workout routine and diet; now add a "glass is half full" mental attitude. Be positive — completely certain — that a good result will happen, and it will.
- **Be confident.** Embrace the chance to succeed at new challenges. Celebrate the one rep max weight. Know that even if you start to feel hungry, you don't need to eat until the next meal.
- **Adjust your attitude.** Change your thinking to positive and your behavior will follow suit.

- **Exhibit determination.** Never give up trying to succeed.
- **Stay focused.** Concentrate on your goals — to keep good form while exercising; to finish the set without giving up midway; to refrain from snacking and sabotaging your diet. Don't be distracted from what you want to achieve.
- **Be patient.** Forget the gimmicky weight loss plans that promise dramatic results in a short time. Aim for steadily losing 1-2 lbs. per week, week by week, until your weight loss goal is met. Even if you hit a plateau, stay on your planned program and eventually you will accomplish your goal.
- **Set realistic goals.** If you have not had a regular exercise program for many years, you will need to train gradually to achieve your health and fitness goals. It can't be done in a few weeks, no matter how hard you try. Years ago you may have eaten chips and a soda for lunch without consequences. But if you tried that today, you would quickly notice a bad result. You may also mis-remember how fit you were when you were younger, so don't compare today to your younger self. If you had a one rep max of 150 lbs. years ago, don't expect to move to a one rep max of 200 lbs. in a few weeks.
- **Expect success.** Not only will you achieve your health and fitness goals, you will maintain them.

Positive mental attitude = Fitness Results

Components of Your Fitness Results

Three essential components are the foundation of Fitness Results:

- Resistance weight training
- Proper nutrition
- Adequate rest

Wait until those three components are in place and have become second nature before you add other activities such as cardio training or yoga. In a perfect world, you'd have unlimited time to go to the gym and work out; you'd have someone preparing all your meals tailored to your nutrition plan; you'd always get 8-9 hours of sleep at night; and you'd still have time for leisure activities like hiking or bike riding or walking the dog. But since you don't live in a perfect world, focus your first efforts on building the foundation. This is the most efficient, fastest and safest way to achieve your Fitness Results.

I used to recommend daily cardio for people who want to lose weight. Now I don't. Cardio should only be added when the foundation is in place and only if it does not compromise the foundation. Adding cardio too early creates stress because it takes time and has very little weight loss benefit compared to the combination of weight training, nutrition and rest.

If one of your goals is to lose body weight, remember that the way to control body weight is to control caloric intake and to exercise with resistance weight training. When you lose weight, you are losing both fat and muscle. Loss of muscle slows your metabolic rate which means that your resting metabolic rate (RMR) — the amount of calories needed to maintain your weight when you are at rest — becomes lower the more weight you lose. Resistance weight training builds muscle which raises RMR. So by combining weight training with lower caloric intake, you'll increase the proportion of muscle to fat and burn more calories while at rest.

Your RMR gives us a baseline of your basic daily caloric needs. Fitness Results has a machine that determines your RMR and a computer program that calculates your additional daily needs based on activity level. With this, we can find the right level of daily calories for you scientifically, without guesswork.

On his first appointment, I asked my client Mark about his goals and what he would like to achieve by working out. He said, "Look at me. I'm fat but I'm in great cardiovascular condition. I have a stationary bike at home and I ride it for two hours every day at Level 12 – the highest level." I knew immediately what he needed to do. His new program consisted of resistance weight training, some minor adjustments to his diet (like cutting out Diet Coke and French fries) and a drastic change in his stationary bike riding. I said, "Could you ride your bike for only one hour 3-4 days a week at Level 6?" Mark replied, "Of course, but that will be too easy." I told him he was right, then explained why riding the bike two hours a day at Level 12 was causing him to be overweight.

His excessive bike riding was causing three negative things to happen:

1. *Overstimulating his metabolism.* This caused Mark to lose control of his appetite, overeat and destroy what should have been a caloric deficit.
2. *Sustained training at high intensity.* During the bike ride, Mark was burning more muscle than fat, reducing his overall amount of muscle.
3. *Lowering his basal metabolic rate.* This caused even more weight gain.

I told Mark that a weight training program would maximize his muscle mass, bringing his metabolism back in balance and contributing to his overall health and fitness. By reducing the amount of cardio training and its intensity, he would be able to control his appetite and reduce muscle loss to an amount that can be replenished by working out.

Mark couldn't believe how fast his body changed by following the program I laid out for him, and how easy it was to get into textbook-perfect health. He learned how to maintain the program on his own and now when I see him, I can tell he has continued to maintain his fitness results.

Three things to remember about Mark's experience:

1. All cardiovascular training is not the same.
2. More is not always better.
3. Harder is not always better.

Mark: 55 years old, 6'0'

6-month comparison

	Beginning training	After 6 months	Change
Weight	247 lbs.	195 lbs.	↓52 lbs.
Body fat percentage	29%	21%	↓8%
Chest	50"	47"	↓8"
Waist	45"	38"	↓8.5"
Hips	44.25"	41.5"	↓3.75
Upper leg	25"	24"	↓1"
Middle leg	23.5"	22"	↓1.5"
Arm	13.5"	13"	↓0.5"

CHAPTER *3*

About Resistance Weight Training

Resistance Weight Training and Weight Loss

Statistics show that without incorporating resistance weight training into a weight loss program, most people will re-gain on average 20% more weight back after a period of weight loss. However, with a resistance weight training program, you are continually stressing your muscles, stimulating them to replace the muscle lost during weight loss. A healthy weight loss program averages 1-2 lbs. per week for both men and women. Avoid any weight loss program claiming faster loss as it can leave you with a higher body fat percentage and result in yo-yo dieting into obesity. (High-intensity cardio can produce the same result).

Here's an example of what happens during a weight loss program without resistance weight training. Assume a 20-year-old woman in good physical condition with 20% body fat decides she wants to lose 10 lbs. She starts a diet but does not combine it with resistance weight training. She loses the desired 10 lbs. (5 lbs. of fat and 5 lbs. of muscle) and her clothes do fit a little better. She is happy to achieve her goal and since she does not want to lose any more weight, she relaxes her diet. Because 5 lbs. of the weight loss was muscle, her RMR is now lower than before, though her body fat percentage remains 20%.

After a time, she is back to eating as she did before the diet and begins gaining weight. Because her RMR is lower, she gains back a total of 12 lbs. (20% more than the 10 lbs. she lost). Her body fat percentage is now 25% because all 12 additional lbs. are fat — she has replaced the 5 lbs. of muscle lost during the diet with 7 lbs. of fat and has lost the shape she had before the diet. With a lower RMR she has trouble keeping her weight under control and so goes back on a diet, starting the cycle all over again. Resistance weight training and proper nutrition changes this unhealthy cycle.

Resistance weight training is especially important for women. Their lower level of testosterone makes it harder to replace and gain muscle compared to men (who are also more genetically designed to gain muscle). Muscle takes up about half the space of fat, so if you lose 5 lbs. of fat and gain 5 lbs. of muscle you will be smaller and have a better shape. You will also increase your RMR and use more energy (calories) to maintain your weight, helping you keep your weight stable. Women don't need to fear gaining muscle — in fact, they should welcome it as a way to have a nicer shape, maintain weight loss and experience overall better health and fitness.

Here is a story for you ladies. My client Joyce was doing great! She had lost 30.5 lbs. and was much healthier. One day at the gym she told me she would have to stop training because her arms were getting too big. She knew that because the sleeves on her shirt seemed tighter than before and tugged on her biceps when she reached for something. I challenged her, claiming that her arms were actually smaller. She bet me $20 that her arms were bigger, and I took the bet. We looked at her starting measurements, then re-measured her arms. In fact, they were 2 inches smaller! (By the way, I did not take collect on the bet even though I had won it fairly. The moral of this story is: don't bet against me!)

Secret #9: Resistance weight training provides a much better awareness of and connection with your body.

Before Joyce started working out, she had no real mind-body connection. Although her shirt sleeves were tighter before she started training, she had no awareness of it. When she started working out, her mind and body connected. During a workout, the brain tells the muscles what to do. For the muscles to perform the task, they require energy. This triggers other functions and results in *muscle pump* – a swelled feeling – and delayed onset muscle soreness (DOMS). These things working in combination provides mind-body connection, leading to better balance and coordination, stronger body, and better brain function.

Another reason Joyce felt that her arms were bigger is that before she started working out and losing weight, her arms had no shape. After losing weight and lifting weights, she gained a nice, feminine muscle tone in her arms for her sleeves to slide over.

Joyce: 53 years old, 5'6"

9-month comparison

	Beginning training	After 9 months	Change
Weight	151.5 lbs.	121 lbs.	↓30.5 lbs.
Body fat percentage	34.8%	26.8%	↓8%
Fat lbs.	52.5 lbs.	36.5 lbs.	↓19 lbs.
Chest	40"	36.5"	↓3.5"
Waist	35"	29"	↓6"
Hips	41"	36"	↓6"
Upper leg	22.5"	19"	↓3.5"
Middle leg	18.75"	16"	↓2.75"
Arm	12.5"	10.5"	↓2"

Resistance Weight Training and Weight Gain

Not everyone wants to lose weight. For some people, being too thin makes them as self-conscious as someone who is overweight. Interestingly, the same program of proper nutrition and workout program will help both overweight and underweight people meet their goals.

Note that the same food will give different people an opposite effect. A food high in sugar will increase one person's appetite and cause them to consume too many calories. The same food for someone else increases their energy level instead of appetite and causes them to burn more calories. (A good fidgeter can burn as many calories in a day as someone running 6 miles).

For those who want to gain muscle size, there is no formula or rate to predict the amount of gain. Each person will gain muscle at a different rate. I set 4-6 lbs. a year as a good goal, followed by 4-6 lbs. the next year for a total of 8-12 lbs. of muscle. This is a significant amount and provides a good base upon which to build.

My client Austin was a freshman in high school when he started training. He was very thin and self-conscious. One day he came into the gym with a big bag of Swedish fish candy – his favorite. – and a 2-liter bottle of soda. I gave him a bad time for bringing that stuff into the gym and then reminded him that if he eats that type of food, his potential to meet his goals will be compromised. (Again, it is all about choices, and it's up to each person to make their own choices. I don't judge. I educate and motivate.)

I trained Austin until he started college. While he was training, he would gain muscle and size if he stopped eating junk food, but get thinner if he started eating it again. The good news is he made good choices most of the time, gained muscle and size, and gained self-esteem and a confident attitude.

Secret #10: I recommend a properly balanced diet of natural food no matter what your health and fitness goals are.

A side story about Austin is that he worked out with his mother. His mom cherished the time they spent together in the gym with me. I have trained many combinations of child and parent – sons and moms, dads and daughters, grandparents and grandchildren – so I hear how much they appreciate the opportunity they had to work out together. Sometimes it was the only thing that kept them connected. I am blessed to have been a part of that.

Here is a story from Austin's mother Karen:

In 2003 when my son Austin was only 13 years old and already 5'11", he was desperately seeking a passion and yearned to gain muscle on his tall frame. I sought out Lance at Fitness Results after hearing about the positive experiences of my friends who trained with him. Lance happily accepted the challenge and took a personal interest in helping Austin achieve his goals. Austin was dedicated, never missed a session, and continued to train with Lance until he left for college, incredibly fit and muscular at 6'4".

In 2006, soon after Austin turned 16 and I was in my late 40s, he and Lance "allowed" me to join them in their training program. I've always felt it is important to maintain health, although I was not a fitness nut. My true passion is showing my Arabian horses. I travel all over the United States from February to October, competing in national Arabian horse shows. This is a sport requiring great agility, stamina and strength which I needed to be a competitive rider. After discussing my goals with Lance, I knew his professional guidance was necessary for a life change.

The training Lance developed to support my goals have proved successful. I am proud to share that in 2007 and 2008, I won the U.S. National Arabian Championship title. This is something I never believed I had the capacity to achieve. I truly owe my success to the program Lance designed to better my performance, and his personal dedication to my fitness.

Now, when I am not riding my horses, me, my husband, all of my children, and even my grandchild will be training with Lance at Fitness Results. A very special thank you from our family to Lance and the Fitness Results family.

Left: Karen and her horse Nicholas. **Right:** Karen's 26-year-old son Austin after winning skid plate race at Irwindale Speedway.

The Importance of Assessments

Before beginning resistance weight training for muscle gain, it is important to have assessments scale, circumference measurements, and a body fat test. This establishes a baseline against which to track how much muscle you are gaining rather than weight. (Weight gain could be a combination of fat and muscle.)

The three foundation elements — resistance weight training, proper nutrition and adequate rest — are just as important for weight gain as weight loss. Gaining muscle is not easy. Some people, often women, say they are afraid to attempt heavy lifts because they do not want to build too much muscle and get too big. You don't need to fear this. It takes a lot of work for both men and women to gain muscle. A weight training program should be something you continue all your life for Fitness Results.

CHAPTER 4

Nutrition and Weight Loss

A common health and fitness program goal is to lose weight. The most effective way to do this is to control your caloric intake and exercise with resistance weight training. If you eat fewer calories than needed to maintain your body weight, you will always lose weight. It is that simple.

Secret #11: Everyone can lose weight by consuming fewer calories. Every 3500-calorie deficit is one pound of weight loss.

Calories will affect the body differently. Calories with little nutrient value (sometimes called "empty calories") can affect your energy level and make you feel sluggish, make it harder to control your appetite, hinder muscle development, and contribute to osteoporosis. Other calories have the reverse effect.

Your resting metabolic rate (RMR) is the amount of calories needed to maintain your weight when you are at rest. You also require calories for activities, and the combination of this and RMR determines the total amount of calories needed daily to maintain your current body weight. A savings of 3500 calories will result in a 1 lb. weight loss. So to lose a pound a week, reduce your intake by 500 calories per day.

Think of calories as a budget to spend on food. If you need to lose weight, then you haven't been spending wisely and will need to strictly adhere to your budget until you reach your weight goal. Then you can adjust your budget to maintenance — the number of calories to maintain your new weight level. A typical maintenance level starting point for women is 1200 calories per day; for men, 1500. As time goes on, the scale will tell you whether you need to make adjustments from the starting point.

It is important to spend your calorie budget on a balance of protein, carbohydrates and fat. I recommend 30% of calories from protein; 40% from carbohydrates; and 30% from fat. Fiber is an important element of nutrition, so eat 20-30 grams of fiber per day (women) and 25-35 grams (men). The reason I emphasize fiber is that it will help you incorporate higher fiber fruits and vegetables as part of your carbohydrate budget allotment. This is particularly beneficial if you are trying to control hunger.

If you have diligently stuck to your daily caloric allotment but have not lost any weight in three or four weeks, reduce your daily caloric intake by 100-200 calories per day until you see weight loss. To stop weight loss, add 100-200 calories per day.

Secret #12: You can lie to yourself but you cannot lie to the scale.

A new client claimed she could not lose weight even though she had tried everything. I didn't say anything, though I was tempted to say that she hadn't tried everything because she hadn't tried eating less (LOL). I didn't say that because I understand the science is easy but the application is hard. That's why I use the art of weight loss, which I will discuss later.

Laurel was large-framed and weighed 235 lbs. From that I knew she had a fairly high metabolic rate. At her first appointment I recommended that she keep her daily caloric intake at no more than 1200 calories consisting mainly of whole, natural foods. It worked! She lost 20 lbs. in about 10 weeks before her weight leveled off. Her initial goal was to lose more than 20 lbs. I explained that the reason she had leveled off and stopped losing weight was because she was moving less weight now than when she started, even taking into account that she was doing resistance weight training. It is not likely that she would lose 2 lbs. of fat and muscle on her diet, then gain back 1 lb. of muscle from weight training.

When you lose weight, you lose both fat and muscle which slows your metabolism. To illustrate: imagine carrying a 20-lb. backpack for 24 hours a day. If you take the backpack off, you will automatically burn fewer calories. So to continue losing weight, you will have to reduce your daily caloric intake. (An aside: when monitoring your weight, do not worry about a single day's result. Look at the trend over time, like a stock chart.)

I recommended Laurel reduce her daily caloric intake by 200 calories a day, to 1000 calories. After doing this, she lost a pound or two, then leveled off again. So every few weeks, I suggested she reduce her intake by another 200 calories.

At the Monday morning weigh-in when the scale showed no weight loss, Laurel would say things like, "I don't think I'm eating enough and that's why I'm not losing any weight" or tell me she had read an article or watched a TV program that said if a person doesn't eat enough, they won't lose weight. Every week I would re-explain that the reason for no weight loss is that she was eating too many calories.

Eventually her food journal showed that she was down to 600 calories a day of mostly whole, natural foods. Yet her rate of weight loss was less than 1 lb. a month. If Laurel was indeed eating only 600 calories a day (which, by the way, I do not recommend), she would be losing weight. When Laurel complained that 600 calories a day was neither safe nor healthy, I knew she was eating way more than that. Of course she swore her journal was completely accurate, even though I challenged her claim. In the end, Laurel was not successful because she didn't apply herself to the nutrition plan. But she needed to blame something other than herself for her lack of success.

I have a machine that measures basal metabolic rate (BMR) and a computer program that calculates additional caloric needs for the day based on daily activities. Laurel agreed to take the test and her BMR was 1600 – very high, especially for a woman, but right where I thought it would be. Now let's do the math: if she was eating 600 calories a day and did not move, she would have had a weekly caloric deficit of 7000 calories which equates to a 2-lb. weekly weight loss. If we added in calories used for movement, exercise and other daily activities, there would be even more weight loss each week. So you can kid yourself and kid me, but you can't fool the scale.

I would like to explain my strategy of periodically reducing caloric intake by 200 calories. When Laurel started with me, I knew she was in denial about her daily caloric intake. Even though I recommended a daily baseline of 1200 calories, I knew she was eating more than that – I estimated 2000 to 2200 calories per day. By suggesting a decrease of 200 calories, I expected she would reduce her intake to 1800-2000 calories. It worked for a while, but because she read articles and listened to friends and TV shows, subconsciously she was journaling fewer calories than she was actually eating. I hoped that while she was journaling 600 calories, she would be eating 1400-1600. If she had followed my program and trusted my professional knowledge, the program would have worked perfectly! With a resting metabolic rate (RMR) of 1600, I knew that she needed more than 1000 calories a day and therefore would have continued to lose another 20 lbs. before possibly needing to further reduce her daily caloric intake to continue weight loss.

Laurel did have great success. She lost over 20 lbs., lowered her body fat percentage, lost inches and greatly improved her health and fitness. But if she would have embraced the program instead of being in denial, she could have had a much better life-changing experience. Because she did not want to make the sacrifices and life changes, she made excuses and placed the blame elsewhere. I prefer people to own their decisions and admit they are truly not ready to make the changes needed to meet the goals they set.

Secret #13: To be successful, your willingness to change has to be stronger than your desire to stay the same.

Thinking back on the previous story, you might wonder why I didn't test her RMR right away since I have the equipment. What I have realized is that the RMR value doesn't matter until you keep an accurate food journal. What does matter is your ability to measure and track and journal an accurate calorie count, just as if you were training for a competitive physique contest or were a professional athlete.

Now I want to talk about the art of nutrition versus the science. One client has a master's degree in nutrition and is a registered nutritionist. Even though she knows more about the science of nutrition than I do, I helped her lose 58 lbs. and 9" in her waist by applying the art of nutrition. I pay attention to each person's habits and personality. Some people need to take baby steps, working on just one issue at a time. Others want to understand the importance of journaling, meal planning, meal preparation, setting goals, being accountable to someone else, being weighed by someone else, and weight loss scale trends. Even professionals need help sometime; in fact, everyone can use help sometime.

I have worked with many different kinds of people during more than 100,000 personal training sessions, and I have learned something from each of them. Because of this, I have developed different techniques so everyone can find success.

Secret #14: Don't let your ego stop you from bettering yourself.

I hear this a lot: *I don't need a trainer because I used to play football* or *my son lifts weights, he can help me.* And this is one of my favorite stories: I was with a client and her friend. My client mentioned that I was a world champion weight lifter and suggested the friend start working out with me. The friend said that her son was just like me because he also competed, so the son could train her. The truth is that the son had competed in a few local bodybuilding competitions – certainly not equivalent to my level of competition. Nor was the son a certified trainer, and he didn't have any training experience. Nevertheless, in her mind *weight training* had only one meaning which meant that her son and I must have the same knowledge.

Protein, Carbohydrates, Fat and Weight Loss

Protein is the building block for muscle and also helps you control hunger. But since you can only digest small amounts of protein at a time, it is best to eat small portions throughout the day. Women should eat 20-30 grams per meal and men 30-40 grams per meal.

Carbohydrates are fuel with an expiration time. If your body does not use carbohydrates for energy within a rather short amount of time after eating, then your body will store the excess as fat to be used later for energy. Fruits, vegetables and legumes (such as peas and beans) are not only a great source of carbohydrates, they contain fiber and other nutrients.

Fat is an essential nutrient and is important for proper body function. Fats provide essential fatty acids, a substance not made by the body, which is important for controlling hunger and for blood clotting and brain development. Fat helps to insulate the body and aids in absorbing vitamins A, D, E and K in the bloodstream. Fat maintains healthy skin and hair and is the energy source the body turns to when it has used up the calories from carbohydrates (generally, after the first 20 minutes of exercise). But because fat has twice as many calories per gram when compared to protein and carbohydrates (9 versus 4), some people have the mistaken idea that it should be eliminated from the diet. This is not correct. For the greatest health benefits, get your fat calories from unsaturated fats, particularly polyunsaturated and monounsaturated.

A few tips for weight loss:

1. Never snack if you are hungry; eat a meal instead. If you snack, you'll be hungry again right away. If you eat a meal, you'll be satisfied for 2-3 hours.
2. Be aware of the calorie count per portion of salad dressing, sauces, candy, cookies, etc. Use these foods only if it fits your calorie budget.

3. Water fasting is good on occasion, but never longer than 24 hours.

4. Another strategy is to eat all your calories in 8 hours, then fast for 16 hours and do that 2-3 times a week. During the fasting period, drink water.

5. You don't need to count calories if you eat a balanced diet of natural foods. Your body will let you know when you have eaten the right amount.

Balancing Your Meals

This image shows the recommendations of the U.S. Department of Agriculture for a balanced meal. It shows the relative proportions of each nutrition component — protein, carbohydrates (grains, fruits, vegetables) and fat (dairy). When deciding on portions for your meal, always have these key components on your plate.

A good serving of protein is 3-6 ounces, which is about the size of your palm and the thickness of a deck of cards. Choose lean protein sources. Since your body can only absorb a little at a time, it's best to have many small portions throughout the day.

Vegetables should take up the majority of the plate. Vary your vegetables to include a wide range of vitamins, minerals and micronutrients.

Grains (which are complex carbohydrates) provide energy throughout the day and for your workout. Unlike simple carbs (sugars), complex carbs contain a lot more fiber and micronutrients.

If you have calories to spare, you may add fruit or dairy to your meal. To read more about the USDA recommendations, visit their web site: choosemyplate.gov

Reading Nutrition Labels: What to Look For

Serving Size: Nutrition labels are for ONE serving, but many packages may contain more. Look at the serving size and compare it with how much you ate.

If you were to eat two servings, for example, you would double everything on the label (calories, carbs, fat, protein and % DV)

Total Fat: Use this to check the total fat intake as well as the type of fat. To decrease your risk of heart disease, avoid foods with trans-fat. Eat more monounsaturated and polyunsaturated fats than saturated fats. Be sure you eat foods high in Omega-3 fatty acids, which are essential and not mentioned in most labels.

Sodium: Limit sodium to help reduce the risk of high blood pressure.

Total Carbohydrate: Check this to see how many grams of carbs you are consuming per serving. Carbs are 4 calories per gram. Soluble and insoluble fiber as well as sugar is considered carbohydrates.

Ingredients: Read the ingredient list. If you can't pronounce an ingredient, it is likely a processed food. Look for foods with the fewest possible ingredients.

% Daily Value (% DV): This is the key to the food's nutritional value. See if this food is giving your body the energy and nutrients it needs to function. *Daily value* is based on the total percentage of that nutrient you need for the day. The * is a reminder that % DV is based on a 2,000 or 2,500 calorie diet.

Nutrition Facts		
8 servings per container		
Serving size		**2/3 cup (55g)**
Amount per serving		
Calories		**230**
		% Daily Value*
Total Fat 8g		**10%**
Saturated Fat 1g		**5%**
Trans Fat 0g		
Cholesterol 0mg		**0%**
Sodium 160mg		**7%**
Total Carbohydrate 37g		**13%**
Dietary Fiber 4g		**14%**
Total Sugars 12g		
Includes 10g Added Sugars		**20%**
Protein 3g		
Vitamin D 2mcg		10%
Calcium 260mg		20%
Iron 8mg		45%
Potassium 235mg		6%
* The % Daily Value (DV) tells you how much a nutrient in a serving of food contributes to a daily diet. 2,000 calories a day is used for general nutrition advice.		

Hunger and Weight Loss

During your weight loss program, you may at times feel hunger pangs. This is not caused by a lack of calories or inadequate nutrition. Instead, the cramping and grinding feelings in your stomach are caused by a stomach irritation. The irritation could be due to overeating, improper digestion, eating spicy food, combining the wrong types of foods, drinking too much liquid with your meal, exposure to smells of food, advertisements for food, social pressure, lack of sleep, boredom, habits or addiction.

The usual reaction to hunger pangs is to eat. This causes the cramping and grinding to stop temporarily, but it may soon be back. Rather than eating, allow the stomach to rest and recover. Water fasting for as little as 16 hours will give the stomach time to recover and has been shown to have significant benefits. A true need for nutrition (food) is not a feeling of discomfort, but a pleasant desire for food — the feeling that you would like to eat, not that you have to eat.

Another source of hunger pangs is a low blood sugar level brought on by carbohydrate sensitivity. When you overeat carbohydrates you induce hyperglycemia — an elevated blood sugar (or glucose) level. To counter the elevated glucose level, your body produces insulin, a hormone that makes glucose available to the body as energy. The insulin causes the body to stop using stored fat as energy and instead to use the glucose in the blood stream. As the glucose levels in the blood stream drop in response to the insulin, your body switches to hypoglycemia — low blood sugar. Now other hormones are released to raise blood glucose levels, creating a dangerous cycle that can lead to weight gain, irritability, moodiness, a tired or lethargic feeling, and even diabetes.

Avoid carbohydrate sensitivity by eating carbohydrates with high fiber content such as green leafy vegetables, soy beans, peas, beans, green beans, chickpeas and lentils. These carbs are slower to digest and tend not to cause overproduction of insulin, thus helping to control hunger.

Secret #15: Be patient. Trust your program and yourself.

I have a lot of great clients with great stories, though some stand out in my mind more than others. Monique's story shows so many things, it could fit almost anywhere. But I want to share it with you now in its entirety because Monique was a client early in my personal training career. My experience with her provided a lot of learning opportunities that I continue to use with my clients today.

As with all clients, at the initial visit I assessed Monique and we set her goals. Remember that this was taking place more than 20 years ago, when technology tools to count calories and apps to journal didn't exist and even finding the caloric count for foods was challenging. Back then, instead of weighing weekly as we do now, I thought it was best to weigh at the initial assessment, then not weigh again for six weeks. Without the nutrition information we have today, it took a lot longer to learn how to make effective changes to the diet, and I found that weekly weighing could actually have a negative effect on attitude.

After Monique's consultation I asked her to refrain from weighing herself for the next six weeks. I said that at the end of that time I'd weigh her and that if she followed my recommendations, she would lose 6-12 lbs. in the six weeks. She agreed to stay off the scale, but couldn't resist. After one week she got on the scale and found no change from her initial weight. Same thing in Weeks 2 and 3. Now she was a little agitated and declared that the program wasn't working and she wasn't sure she should continue. I reminded her that she didn't have a contract and could stop whenever she wanted, but that at the initial session she had promised to stick with the program for 6 weeks. I also mentioned that I would give her a full refund if she hadn't lost at least six pounds at the end of six weeks.

On the fourth week, she was even more agitated. She had weighed herself and still no weight loss. She declared the program to be a failure. I suggested that since we were so close to the end, she should continue for the last two weeks. On the fifth week, she had lost a few pounds, but not the 6-12 lbs. we were expecting. Again she wasn't sure she wanted to continue, but since there was only one week to go, she stayed.

You guessed it – in Week 6 the scale showed exactly a 12-pound weight loss from the start. At her very next workout, Monique handed me a big stack of money. She told me she had taken out a loan in order to pay for one year of training in advance – that was her way of committing and keeping herself from quitting.

For the next year she did great, with consistent weight loss except for a few hiccups. Once we hit a period where Monique went several weeks without a weight loss. I checked her food journal and asked her about her nutrition plan. I couldn't find any explanation for the stall in weight loss. So I took a closer look and probed a little deeper. I noticed that for breakfast she had eggs, small piece of toast, a little bit of oatmeal and a little cantaloupe. I asked her about the eggs – that checked out. She was having her toast dry, so that wasn't the problem. Then I asked about the cantaloupe. She reiterated that it was a little cantaloupe. I said, "How much is a little cantaloupe? A quarter slice?" She said, "No, a little cantaloupe, about 6" around." That taught me to get very detailed when asking questions about food portions.

I think that deep down, Monique knew that she was kidding herself and eating more than she should. But when I uncovered her definition of *little cantaloupe,* I reminded her that she could only have a small slice – about a quarter of the cantaloupe.

She did get back on track with her weight loss but then she hit another snag. Again, weeks went by without any weight loss. I asked her repeatedly if she was following the program and she said she was doing everything perfectly and couldn't figure out why her weight loss had stopped.

Later that day, my brother called me from a sports bar where he was watching Monday Night Football. He had locked his keys in his car and asked me to bring him his spare car key. When I got to the sports bar, I found Monique sitting at a table eating chips and salsa and drinking a beer. I greeted her and she knew she was busted! At her next gym session she apologized for not being honest about her food intake and swore she would do better in the future.

On Friday of that same week, I took my mom to dinner at her favorite Mexican restaurant to celebrate her birthday. After we were seated, I noticed that Monique and a group of friends were sitting at a table across the restaurant. Again, she was having chips, salsa and a beer. Rather than going over to confront Monique, I thought it would be funny to have the waiter deliver a salad with no dressing to her and tell her "this is from your trainer."

When the salad arrived, Monique burst into tears and immediately left the restaurant without saying anything to anyone. Of course I felt terrible about what I had done and how it had completely backfired. The next time I saw Monique at the gym, I apologized and said that I hadn't meant to be offensive, and in fact, thought it would be funny. I said I always want to be supportive and it is all about her choices. To my surprise, she said she wasn't upset with me but with herself for lying to me. The crying was because she was disappointed in herself. And with that, she was back on track and continued to have great fitness results.

But that's not the end of Monique's story. To show her appreciation for the results I had helped her achieve, she gave me a surprise present on my birthday:

Monique had placed an ad in the local newspaper for Fitness Results. It showed her "before and after" and gave her weight loss over nine months. This was the very first advertisement for Fitness Results, and a very touching way to show her appreciation.

Monique: 27 years old, 5'5"

9-month comparison

	Beginning training	After 9 months	Change
Weight	225 lbs.	151 lbs.	↓70 lbs.
Clothing size	18/20	11/12	↓3 sizes
Chest	40.5"	37"	↓4.5"
Waist	37"	28"	↓9"
Hips	49"	38"	↓11"
Upper leg	28.5"	24"	↓4.5"
Calf	17"	15"	↓2"

Note: after two years, Monique was down to 135 lbs. – a loss of 90 lbs. overall.

Monique trained with me for several more years before getting married, moving out of the area, and having a little girl. I lost track of her for several years but recently re-connected through Facebook. I am very sorry to report that she is now battling cancer. I send prayers and best wishes for Monique and her family in this difficult time.

Your Personality and Weight Loss

When you start on a weight loss program, you need to know your personality type so you will have realistic expectations.

All-or-nothing personality. This personality type decides to do something and gives it 100%, unless they can't — and then they don't try at all. On the plus side, this person will start a weight loss program by planning meals carefully, keeping a food journal, and strictly following the weight loss program. This brings instant success as long as the plan is being following. But an interruption (such as going on vacation) means a time to relax and a free-for-all with no restrictions. If this sounds like you, acknowledge it and include some structure on your vacation so you can continue on your path to success.

Ease-in personality. This personality type eases into a program with baby steps by picking a single problem (like drinking soda all day or eating a big bowl of ice cream every night) and getting it under control before moving on to the next one. This person might take a little longer to see results, but can usually stay on track for a long time.

In-denial personality. This personality claims to be doing everything right, but won't allow any verification — no review of the food journal or meal plan, for instance. Another characteristic is to have many excuses for why the program isn't working.

Some people blame their inability to lose weight on a low resting metabolic rate (RMR) or a thyroid problem. (This can make weight loss more challenging but still possible.) It is true that very rapid weight loss (more than 1-2 lbs. per week for women and 3-5 lbs. per week for men) lowers your RMR as your body conserves calories, and can make you feel lethargic. But a healthy program of weight loss consisting of eating fewer calories per day than your body requires, combined with resistance weight training, will produce results.

No matter what your personality type, if you eat fewer calories than needed to maintain your weight, you will lose weight.

It always works, and it's that simple.

Body Mass Index and Weight Loss

Body Mass Index (BMI or Quetelet Index) is a health assessment tool you may be familiar with. BMI was first presented in 1835 by a mathematician, not a doctor, to quantify an average man in a given population. The BMI calculation is simple and gives a value based on body weight. In large populations, BMI correlates with body fat percentage for the population, but is not reliable for individuals within the population. In fact, individuals with the same BMI value could have as much as a 15% variance in actual body fat.

At Fitness Results, we use a measure that is suitable for individuals — percent of body fat. This measure has only a 2% +/- variance. When used with other assessment tools such as body weight and circumference measurements, and subjective measures such as how you look and feel in your clothes, percent of body fat is a much better way than BMI to assess overall health.

The healthiest body fat percentages are in the range of 12% to 22% for women and 9% to 19% for men. Women with a body fat percentage of 23% to 29% and men with a body fat percentage of 20% to 29% are considered somewhat healthy. A body fat percentage of 30% or greater is considered obese for both men and women. Beginning at age 60, for both men and women, the body fat percentage ranges increase by 2% for each decade.

Weight Loss Program Tips

1. **Eat balanced meals.** At each meal, aim for 30% protein, 40% high-fiber carbohydrates and 30% fat. A balanced meal should keep you full for at least 3-4 hours.
2. **Eat high-fiber carbohydrates.** Women should have 20-30 grams of fiber a day; men should have 25-35 grams.
3. **Eat before you get hungry.** Space your meals so you eat before you are really hungry (minimum intervals of 2½ to 3 hours).
4. **Plan your meals in advance, up to one week ahead.** This will help you maintain a balanced food budget.
5. **Keep a food journal.** Writing down exactly what you eat will help you identify small things that may be sabotaging your program.
6. **Use smaller plates.** Your food portions will appear larger on a small plate.
7. **Eat whole fruit instead of drinking juice.** Juicing concentrates carbohydrates and removes fiber from fruit.
8. **Combine foods to enhance flavors.** Plain oatmeal is healthy but uninteresting. Add some blueberries and sliced almonds (which also adds fiber) to perk up the oatmeal. But be careful not to increase the overall calorie count of the meal or to eat more because it tastes good.
9. **Avoid snacking.** If you are hungry, eat a meal. After a snack you will soon feel hungry again.

10. **Avoid empty-calorie foods.** Candy, donuts, alcohol, cookies, cake, and pie are a few examples of empty-calorie foods. Eat nutritious food that keeps your metabolic rate up, supports muscle development and promotes overall good health.

11. **Avoid some kinds of foods.** Stay away from meat and vegetables that are battered or crusted then fried. Don't use artificial sweeteners or beverages that contain them. Avoid processed foods (they are both high in calories and high in sodium).

12. **Identify your causes of overeating.** Learn whether you have triggers like stress, boredom, overeating at social functions, or cravings for sweets, salt, or fat.

13. **Do not overeat because you are trying too hard to eat healthy food.** We are bombarded with ads, news reports and studies telling us what to eat to be healthy or prevent illness. We start adding foods to our diet but do not cut back on what we were already eating. So we end up consuming too many calories in our quest to be healthy. Think about this: you can only live a few minutes without air; you can live a few days without water; but you can live for weeks without food.

14. **If you get rid of one bad habit or food, do not replace it.** Don't give up ice cream and have cookies.

15. **Use your support group.** Your personal trainer, the people in your group fitness program, and others will all encourage you.

An Automotive Analogy for How Fat Works

To help you understand how fat works in the body, let's play a game of pretend. You are now a car – a sexy, Italian sports car with timeless beauty and peak performance.

To keep your showroom appearance and maintain the ability to achieve at peak performance, you need three things: vital fluids; regular maintenance; and responsible driving.

For you to function, you have to add fuel regularly. Eating food is like going to the gas station to refuel. Since you are a high performance sports car, picking the right fuel blend is crucial. You require a high octane fuel to perform at peak levels. If you don't use the right fuel, you can hinder performance and perhaps cause damage.

You need an adequate amount of protein to supply the horsepower for power. You can use muscle for fuel but you're better off using carbohydrates and fat. Combined, the two become the ultimate source of fuel.

Fat, a great source of fuel for peak performance, is also used for all the operating systems and to keep the exterior showroom new. Carbohydrates mainly function as fuel that spares the use of protein and fat for other important functions like performing at peak performance and maintaining a sexy appearance.

So what happens if you use bad fuel? You will feel sluggish, you may stall, you might not start and you'll have to go to the mechanic for a checkup. For peak performance and the ability to go the distance, you need good fuel!

Even if you're using the right kind of fuel, you can put too much in the gas tank. In that case, the extra weight from the excess fuel produces sluggishness, the inability to take sharp turns, compromises to acceleration and braking, and loss of that sexy sports car appearance. Eventually, as you keep overfilling the gas tank, you'll look and feel like a tired sedan. You'll be carrying around a growing amount of extra fuel that you never use because you are parked in the garage instead of getting out for fun drives. And yet by habit, you'll keep adding more fuel.

Sometimes you might switch to cheap fuel or fuel with the wrong mix, believing that doesn't really matter because everyone else is doing the same thing. After a while, the bad fuel or mix may lull you into being satisfied with being a tired sedan rather than the sexy sports car you used to be. You may get used to running poorly, having no power, and being in the repair shop all the time.

Now imagine that you're filling the gas tank and the automatic shutoff valve doesn't work. Instead of the fuel flow stopping when the tank is full, the fuel overflows the tank into a second, third or fourth gas tank that you didn't even know you had. You keep filling the main tank, even though common sense and the fuel tabulation dial says you've exceeded tank capacity.

You may be afraid to stop putting in fuel because you don't want to risk running out of gas and you don't realize the automatic shutoff valve is broken. You keep filling the tank until eventually you realize you should quit adding fuel. This scenario – thinking you need fuel, overfilling the tank because you don't know the automatic shutoff valve is broken and that there are extra fuel tanks, and measuring the amount of fuel to add by what you added last time – repeats itself in a dangerous cycle. After an extended period of overfueling, you feel tired, sluggish and unwell. You look different as a result of carrying around too much fuel in the main and hidden fuel tanks.

Fat cells in your body are like little fuel tanks. The bigger the reserve of fat, the more volume the cells take up; the smaller the reserve of fat, the less volume in the cells. Just like the fuel in the gas tank that is used, then expelled through the tailpipe, when you lose weight, the excess fuel leaves as you are breathing. It doesn't leave because of a cleansing diet, which has the same effect as going to a car wash. The car looks nice and clean but the washing had no effect on amount of fuel in the gas tank.

Secret #16: The key to reducing stored fuel is to begin using the best blend of fuel and to get out and drive.

Here are a few common mistakes people make to reduce the excess stored fuel.

1. *Reducing the amount of fuel added but neglecting the engine and operating systems.* If you stop adding excess fuel until you reach a desired level, you will reduce the overall amount of stored fuel. But you won't be operating at peak performance and you'll still be sluggish, tired, and have all the same issues as before losing the excess fuel. Even worse, you'll be at risk of re-starting the cycle of overfueling, perhaps even exceeding the previous levels of excess fuel.

Stopping the cycle of adding excess fuel isn't enough; you also have to tune up the engine and operating systems.

2. *Copying the person who hits the highway and runs all-out for two hours every day to meet a fuel reduction goal.* If an engine and operating system that hasn't been properly maintained is called on to deliver sustained peak performance, something will fail. Running all-out for longer than a few seconds at a time without a short break in between means that the stored fuel can't keep up with the demand for quality and a proper mix. Instead, the fuel will come from the vital fluids needed to maintain performance. So during the process of lowering excess fuel, you'll sacrifice performance at a faster rate than you use up fuel.

3. *Giving in to the temptation to add fuel because you've just used up a lot.* After being out on the highway, you may feel the need to refuel. If you do so, you will be negating the fuel reduction that came from the highway run, hindering future performance and exacerbating the existing poor performance.

The key to reducing excess stored fuel is to add the proper blend of fuel, stopping just short of filling the tank. This works because you are running mostly on high performance fuel, mixed with some of the stored, lower-quality fuel. Over time, with proper care and maintenance, performance will improve and you can attain the original showroom condition.

I choose this analogy between car fueling for peak performance and the combination of human body nutrition, diet and exercise to simplify a complicated process. I hope I have made it easier for you to understand.

Supplements and Your Fitness Results

Think of supplements as an insurance policy rather than the main component to achieve your fitness results. The name says it all: *supplements.* They supplement the nutritional components of your caloric intake of natural food.

I was visiting the business of one of my clients and was asked a question by the receptionists – two women in their 20s. Knowing I was a personal trainer, one wanted to know my thoughts on branch chain amino acids (BCAA) because she had heard that BCAAs are good for weight loss and energy. The other receptionist asked my opinion about the best all-around supplement to have more energy and lose weight.

I answered that I needed to know more about why they felt low on energy before I could make any recommendations and noted that they were expecting a supplement to be the main path to their health and fitness goals. To make my point, I asked if they had car insurance, which they did. I told them to think of supplements as they did their car insurance. Do everything you can to meet the nutrition needs that support your health and fitness goals, then add supplements of nutrients that are important but might not be present in sufficient amounts based on their natural food intake and life style. Even though you have car insurance that will pay for damage from a crash, you don't drive recklessly. You drive safely and hope you are not in an accident. The insurance gives you peace of mind knowing that if you do have an accident, you can recover. Both receptionists got my point and said they would come to the gym for a free consultation.

This story demonstrates the effect of clever advertising aimed at people looking for an easy fix. Yes, supplements are beneficial but should be used as insurance, not as the main road to health and fitness.

Secret #17: If it sounds too good to be true, it is.

Ever heard of snake oil? It is something sold as a remedy but not really useful or helpful in any way. The diet and weight loss industry is full of snake oil salesmen offering a magic pill that produces unbelievable results. But could these results be due to the placebo effect – that is, the person's belief in the treatment rather than any attributes of the product itself

It's easy to be seduced by the glitz and glamour and seductive sales pitch of a snake oil salesman. Don't be taken in by the hype. You are buying a consumable product, so if you value your health, know exactly what you are putting in your body. Make sure the product supports your health and fitness goals and is within your financial budget.

In the discussion of supplements, I mentioned using them as an adjunct to a diet of natural foods. Many people who decide to use a supplement think that purchasing them at a health food or nutrition store guarantees that the product will be safe and beneficial. It doesn't.

Although I am not a chemist or doctor or analytic expert in over-the-counter (OTC) supplements, I have a solid basis of knowledge regarding supplements sold in nutrition and health food stores. I know it can be confusing to find the right product, so I recommend that you check with your doctor before adding any supplement to your diet. Just like with prescription medication, if you take several OTC products simultaneously, you may be unintentionally "overdosing" on a particular ingredient. This isn't safe. For example, taking an energy-enhancing product or a weight loss product as directed should be safe. But taking them in combination may not be. Be sure to do adequate research and use common sense so you can make an educated decision based upon your specific needs and goals.

I am not categorically opposed to using supplements. I am opposed to using them without first evaluating my client's lifestyle, health and fitness and discussing the pros and cons of the product. Here's an example of when taking a supplement might be beneficial. Suppose a woman wants to lose weight, so she needs to keep her daily caloric intake low. Her daily calorie allotment of protein may not be high enough to get an adequate amount of protein. So a supplement of protein pills would provide the protein needed to support muscle development without adding calories.

Another example is a person who for some reason (not enough time, no interest) is not engaging in meal planning for one or more meals — typically, breakfast or lunch. Rather than depending on fast food for the meal, I might recommend a meal replacement. While this is not as good as real meal planning, it is a better choice given the circumstances.

A word about some types of products you may find in health food or nutrition stores but are not, strictly speaking, supplements – thermogenic and prohormone products. *Thermogenic* means *tending to produce heat.* The term is often applied to weight loss supplements that claim to speed up your metabolism, boost energy levels and suppress appetite. Be aware that the Food and Drug Administration and many medical professionals say that achieving thermogenesis using supplements is not safe. Because these products increase your heart rate and may block essential nutrition utilization, they are not recommended.

Prohormones products are compounds acting as a chemical precursor to hormones (such as testosterone) and steroids, as well as hormones that counter the negative effects of higher testosterone such as rising estrogen. Among bodybuilders, prohormones are widely used and in demand, which might be an argument in favor of their effectiveness. Some but not all prohormones have been legally banned since 2004. There are companies taking advantage of legal loopholes to sell these products. They use seductive advertising and target consumers looking for a short cut to achieve their fitness goals. This makes it doubly important to do your research and use common sense before deciding to use a prohormone product.

To recap: as long as you make an educated decision based on research and your health and fitness needs, you will find products in the health and nutrition stores that can be a great addition to a health and fitness program.

Nitric Oxide and Your Fitness Results

I became aware of the importance of nitric oxide in training in 1998, the year three American scientists won the Nobel Prize in Medicine *"for their discoveries concerning nitric oxide as a signaling molecule in the cardiovascular system"* ["The Nobel Prize in Physiology or Medicine 1998". Nobelprize.org. Nobel Media AB 2014. Web. 21 Jun 2016. http://www.nobelprize.org/nobel_prizes/medicine/laureates/1998/].

In 1998 I competed and won several competitions, including the World Championship, evidence of my tremendous physical condition. At the time, someone asked if I had ever had a digital pulse analysis done. This is a test that measures how pliable your blood vessels are, and determines your cardiovascular health rather than cardiovascular condition. Pulse wave analysis has been around for hundreds of years; recently, new digital equipment has made it much easier to obtain accurate information.

I was 35 years old, had a healthy lifestyle, and exercised to keep my body as youthful as possible. I had the analysis done and was stunned when my grade indicated that I had tested as if I was 50 years old. My great cardiovascular fitness was certainly not the same as my cardiovascular health.

I didn't like that result at all, even though this is a common finding not only for the general population, but also for health and fitness professionals. We often hear about a seemingly healthy person dying at an abnormally young age of heart attack, and cardiovascular disease is the #1 cause of death in the United States and worldwide.

I took the results of the digital pulse analysis to heart. I purchased a Digital Pulse Analyzer (DPA) so I could track my progress as well as my client's. The machine measures the flexibility of your arteries, including the peripheral ones where the first signs of cardiovascular disease become apparent.

A blood pressure test measures the pressure in your arteries as your heart pumps. The upper number reading is called *systolic*. It measures the pressure as your heart pumps blood during a heartbeat. The lower number is *diastolic* and measures the pressure between heart beats while your heart rests. People who are young and healthy have flexible arteries so when the heart beats and pumps blood into the arteries, it pushes with such force that it sends a shock wave of pulses traveling through the arteries. The force acts like an extension of the heart, pulsing to help circulate blood and giving the heart extra time to rest before the next beat is required. The greater the arterial flexibility, the less stress on the cardiovascular system.

As we age, our arteries become less flexible and stiffen, losing the reverberation (expansion and contraction) of the shock wave pulses. The heart has to work harder to force the blood throughout the body and gets less rest between beats. In addition, plaque (fatty deposits) may begin sticking to the artery walls, accumulating to cause narrowing of the arterial space and even more cardiovascular stress. Now we are at even greater risk for cardiovascular and other diseases.

The peripheral arteries provide blood to your extremities and are the smallest in the body. Even the slightest reduction in flexibility or circumference can have a dramatic effect on circulation and more quickly become complete blockage. The DPA machine can measure arterial flexibility even in the smallest peripheral arteries, serving as an early detection device for stroke and diabetes.

Next I began studying to find out how to improve my cardiovascular health. I discovered that nitric oxide has been shown to reduce high blood pressure and is believed to restore arterial flexibility by repairing the endothelium (the inner lining of an artery responsible for its flexibility). While this theory has not yet been proven, it may be soon.

Nitric oxide is very popular with bodybuilders because it is a vasodilator, meaning it increases blood flow. Bodybuilders like to talk about *the pump* and how nitric oxide gives you a better *pump*. By itself, this doesn't mean anything and could actually be detrimental if you "chase the pump" and overtrain. *Chasing the pump* means thinking that more sets or more reps will produce a better pump or fullness feeling, leading to better muscle development. But having a good pump doesn't mean you have achieved a good workout, and not having a good pump doesn't mean you didn't achieve a good workout.

Vasodilation helps with muscle development by increasing blood flow to the muscle and brain for better neurotransmission and other benefits associated with increased blood flow. More blood means more fuel to work harder and longer before you hit your failure point; the ability to achieve a new max rep or get in an extra rep. Cumulatively over time, if you can work a little harder, you will see faster muscle and strength gains. Another advantage of vasodilation is better recovery after a working set for the next set, and better recovery after the workout so the muscles recover and adapt, preparing for the next workout.

L-arginine is an amino acid that is one of the basic building blocks of proteins. L-arginine converts to nitric oxide and was the first amino acid used in supplements to promote nitric oxide. Like most supplements, you couldn't prove it was working but had to hope it was. I began using L-arginine supplements for my cardiovascular health. I also changed my diet to include more vegetables, and checked progress with the DPA machine. I began to see some changes. A company called Berkeley came out with nitric oxide test strips and that changed everything. I was able to test and immediately discover what raised my nitric oxide levels.

Simultaneously, the scientific community began learning more about nitric oxide. We now know that a diet of high nitrate foods like arugula, spinach and other dark-green, leafy vegetables, and beetroot juice is the key to maintaining a higher nitric oxide level. Two ounces of beetroot juice can provide the nitric oxide contained in 3 or 4 beets, so it is a convenient way to eat high-nitrate food.

For me, eating high nitrate foods works best to keep my nitric oxide levels up. When you eat high-nitrate foods, your stomach acid breaks them down and recycles them back to your mouth as saliva. When you swallow high-nitrate saliva, it reacts to the bacteria on your tongue to convert nitrate to nitric oxide (a very complex system). Certain mouth washes and chewing gums reduce nitric oxide levels by reducing bacteria on the tongue.

Although I rely most on high-nitrate foods, I do find that supplements containing L-citrulline and L-arginine can give my nitric oxide level a boost. Note that if you are over 40 years old, L-arginine supposedly does not convert nitrates to nitric oxide, so you are advised to use L-citrulline instead. Personally I don't see any difference even though I am over 50 years old. I get the same benefits from either L-arginine or L-citrulline. Neither alone raises my nitric oxide to a substantial level; it has to be paired with my high-nitrate diet to achieve a high beneficial level.

Secret #18: High-nitrate foods increase your nitric oxide levels and nitric oxide helps heal cardiovascular disease.

High nitrate vegetables include arugula, bok choy, cabbage, carrots, celery, collard greens, green beans, lettuce, parsley, radishes, red beets and red beet juice, spinach, and Swiss chard.

Secret #19: Nitric oxide can increase performance in all sports.

Nitric oxide helps bodybuilders, weight lifters, and all other athletes. It is one of the best-kept secrets in sports. I read a study reporting that world class runners and cyclists who drank two cups of beetroot juice average more than 10% increase in performance. That's huge! Athletes at that level who don't drink beetroot juice could train for a year without making a 10% increase.

One morning I was hiking with my wife and her sister-in-law Judy who was complaining about lack of energy on the hike. I told her about the beetroot juice and the next morning had her drink some before we started that day's hike. We used the same trail, which Judy reported was easier going than on the previous day. She also said she felt much better.

Judy, an avid tennis player, mentioned that one woman consistently beat her because Judy got tired toward the end of the match while the other woman didn't. I suggested that Judy drink two cups of beetroot juice about 1 ½ or two hours before the next tennis match. A few weeks later, Judy called, excited to say she took my suggestion and finally won a match against the other woman. Now she calls beetroot juice her secret weapon. She is playing much better and winning many more matches.

Using nitric oxide means you don't have to work as hard to achieve the same level of performance as you would without it. Therefore, you can accomplish even more, achieve greater performance, and maintain cardiovascular health and conditioning.

Secret #20: Adequate rest is crucial for a healthy mind and body.

Sleep is crucial for a healthy body, mind and active lifestyle. In fact, it is just as important as exercise and a nutrition plan for reaching your Fitness Results. I recommend getting 7-9 hours of sleep per night.

A quality night's rest

- repairs muscle fibers that were damaged from an intense weight lifting session;
- reduces inflammation;
- increases immune function;
- restores mental and physical fatigue; and
- rebalances your hormones.

If meeting the sleep requirement is difficult, keep this in mind: studies show that 20-30 minute naps can help restore your body's hormone levels similar to a night's rest.

One of my biggest regrets about the years when I was competing is that I sacrificed sleep to get in a workout. I wish I had done a better job of balancing exercise and rest in my health and fitness program. I am convinced that the reason I get little muscle tears these days is because I didn't get enough sleep to let my muscles adequately recover and heal between workouts. I am sure I have some scar tissue buildup due to lack of proper recovery time. Even though I can still lift a very respectable amount of weight, especially for my age, I have occasionally experienced a muscle tear while lifting a weight that would have been a warmup a few years ago. The only benefit of my experience is that I can now share what I learned with you.

If you find you can't sleep, then substitute meditation in a quiet place with just you and your thoughts. The familiar benefits of meditation include stress relief, self-awareness, and better concentration. Meditation also seems to help muscle recovery after exercise by reducing overstimulation of nerve signals, allowing muscles to recover faster.

CHAPTER 5

My Workout Philosophy

An effective workout is based on a plan that includes the number of days per week that you will work out, what muscle groups will be trained each day, what you accomplished in both maximum pounds and repetitions in previous sessions for the muscle group, and the training goal for this workout session (such as a new one rep max or more reps with a set weight). I have provided example workout plans for 2, 3, 4 and 5 sessions per week.

For most people, I recommend three workouts per week because it is a fast, safe and efficient way to produce Fitness Results. Training three days a week will double the benefit you'll get over two days per week. Training four or five days per week will produce greater benefit than three days per week, but the benefit is incremental and not as dramatic as the difference between a two-day weekly workout and a three-day weekly workout.

However, your workout plan must be flexible. If your plan for the day was to achieve a new one rep max on the bench press but during warm up you experience shoulder pain that doesn't go away, then you'll need to change your plan in response. Don't give up training the muscle group; instead, switch to dumbbells and change the angle of your hands so you can work the muscle group without shoulder pain. Balancing risks and rewards will help you achieve a better workout no matter what your goals and fitness level.

There is always more than one way to train a muscle group. Your job is to select the method that is safe and minimizes the risk of injury. For example, one way to do a lat pull down exercise is to pull the bar down behind your neck. Another way is to pull it down with the bar in front of your body. Both movements work the muscles in the same way. But pulling the bar down behind your neck adds stress to the neck and shoulders and could increase the risk of injury. Pulling the bar down in front avoids this problem. It is simple common sense to train using an exercise that is safer and is just as effective on the target muscle group.

Another example is barbell squats for training your legs and lower body. Rather than resting the barbell on your upper back and neck and stressing your shoulders by making them bear the weight of the bar, use a set of shoulder pads. Or use a leg press or hack squat machine to train the legs. These machines provide stability and comfort with just a small sacrifice of training results. On balance you will have much less risk of injury.

You will not be able to train if you are injured or in pain. So constantly evaluate the risk you are taking against the potential reward. Decide in favor of safety and you'll be able to exercise for years to come.

Your Workout Goals

For most people, the goal of the workout is to look better and feel better. This is very different from the goal of a competitive athlete who is training for peak performance. The athlete's exercise program is based on a level of intensity, duration, commitment and risk-taking required to achieve top performance. The athlete takes years to reach a performance level and the effort to attain each new level of performance increases exponentially, like the Richter Scale for measuring an earthquake. To increase his strength, the athlete has to sustain the work it took to get to the present level, then add even more to reach the new level.

Your program needs to fit your age, current fitness level, health assessment, goals and commitment. You can't adopt or modify someone else's program and achieve their results or even a fraction of their results. Working someone else's program — especially an aggressive one like a competitive athlete's — means you're adding stress, spending more time, increasing the risk of pain and injury and achieving sub-par results. The same is true for celebrity-endorsed workouts or the latest fad workout. If the promise of the workout sounds too good to be true, it proves that it is.

If you were an athlete in your teens and 20s, don't set a goal today that matches what you were able to do then. Today you are older and less fit and you are training to look and feel better, not for peak athletic performance.

Tailor your training program to produce maximum results based on your age, gender, fitness level, overall health and training goals. Because your program is custom to you, it will produce results faster and with less risk and discomfort. All you have to do is perform the exercises using good form and with sincere commitment to improve.

People who say that using a traditional weight training method is boring may have that opinion because they are not working out correctly or don't understand that they can improve just by making changes to the amount of weight or reps or rest as needed. Workouts can have infinite variations, creating advancements that make your fitness and health programs both rewarding and fun.

If you train using a personal program and do your workouts with good form, intensity, pace, duration and recovery, your body will respond. I've seen this happen more than once: a client who has been working out consistently but overly aggressive is nevertheless seeing slow improvements. I drop the workout pace, reduce the amount of sets, and pay close attention to proper form. The client is skeptical because the workout doesn't seem as hard or intense as before. At the same time, I don't let the client give up or quit until totally fatigued. This results in an improved level of tolerance for hard work. Suddenly there are huge improvements in strength and muscle gain. In as little as two months, I've seen up to 18 lbs. of muscle gain and reduced body fat percentage before leveling off to a slower rate of gain. By using the right combination of training program and effective workouts, the body will tap into its pent-up potential.

Equipment Used During Your Workout

Equipment typically used during a workout includes barbells, dumbbells, weight machines, suspension trainer, resistance band and your own body weight. By varying the equipment used for training you can change the stress level for your muscles.

Each piece of equipment has strengths and weaknesses. It is helpful to know them so you can make good decisions about changing equipment.

- **Dumbbells**
  Strength: maximum coordination and stability; works all supporting muscles.
  Weakness: your coordination can limit the amount of weight you can move. It helps to have a spotter.

- **Weight machines**
  Strength: permits you to focus on lifting the weight without worrying whether the weight will fall on you.
  Weakness: minimal coordination and stability; does not work the supporting muscles.

- **Barbells**
  Strength: some coordination and stability; works supportive muscles when using heavy weight.
  Weakness: your coordination may limit the amount of weight you can move. You should have a spotter.

Suspension Training and Pilates

Muscle development is nature's way of coping with the stress of gravity by developing stronger and bigger muscles to overcome gravity's effect. Suspension training uses the body's own weight to provide resistance against gravity, while Pilates uses manmade springs. Suspension training and Pilates equipment are similar in the way the exercises are performed and both add greater instability than dumbbells.

As mentioned, suspension training uses your body weight to provide resistance against gravity. This makes the limit of resistance equal to your body weight. You can still change reps and rest to add more difficulty.

Suspension training equipment is lightweight and portable and allows you to perform many exercises. Some muscle groups are more suited for suspension training than others, such as all core exercises and all rowing exercises for back; and rear deltoids. Suspension training is not as good for chest exercises as most people find it awkward. If you are strong enough for chest exercises not to be awkward, they won't be challenging enough. Using suspension training for legs works for those who are badly out of shape. But with a little advancement, the exercise is no longer challenging. Only those who are very advanced can maximally work the latissimus dorsi back muscles with suspension training.

Because the workout is defined by your body weight, distance away from the anchor point, and form, improvement is difficult to assess and is largely subjective. The instability of suspension training results in a longer learning curve to be able to perform most exercises safely and well.

Suspension training was invented by former Navy Seal Randy Hetrick, and is a great training tool for the military. The suspension device can be attached to many different things like a tree branch or other support, allowing a soldier to maintain physical fitness in a jungle or submarine or other field operations location. Those who are called upon to fight for their lives and the lives of others will be better conditioned because of suspension training. Upon returning to home base, soldiers will have access to other exercise equipment and can resume resistance weigh training.

- **Suspension training**

  Strength: lightweight; portable; allows you to perform a variety of exercises (though some muscle groups respond better than others); more effective and efficient than Pilates.

  Weakness: limited by your body weight; no defining weight, making it difficult to assess improvement; has a longer learning curve to perform exercises safely and well.

Unlike suspension training, Pilates uses manmade springs as resistance against gravity. The tension in the springs can be changed, making it easier to measure improvement in Pilates than in suspension training. Like suspension training, Pilates takes longer to learn proper form and technique.

Pilates was invented by German physical trainer Joseph Hubertus Pilates. While interned in England during World War I as an enemy alien, he used bed springs and straps to provide resistance during exercising. The system worked well and later was adopted by the dance community. This may be the reason Pilates has a reputation for providing balance and flexibility training. However, Pilates is neither safer nor more effective at increasing balance and flexibility than resistance weight training recommended in this book.

- **Pilates**

  Strength: Ability to regulate the tension in the springs; ability to track advancements and set goals.

  Weakness: Takes longer to learn proper form and techniques.

Lest you think I am biased against suspension training and Pilates, I do have both kinds of equipment in my gym and I am certified and trained in their use. If a client wants to use Pilates equipment after a consultation and hearing my recommendations, I honor their choice and provide the best Pilates training possible. Suspension training is great for larger groups that we might not otherwise be able to accommodate in the gym.

On occasion a client will come for a consultation and tell me their doctor said they could exercise using Pilates equipment but not free weights. To me this defies common sense and shows the doctor's lack of knowledge of exercise and tendency to follow trends.

Secret #21: It takes both free weights and machines to train your whole body safely, efficently and effectively.

Regarding the argument over whether free weights are better than machines: again, this violates common sense. Half the muscles of the body work with gravity; the others work against gravity. So to work the whole body, we use machines that manipulate the forces of gravity using cables and pulleys, and we adjust the way the weight is delivered with cams and levers. So it is the combination of free weights and machines that allows us to stress our complete musculoskeletal system and adapt, making us better mentally and physically while remaining safe.

Secret #22: The more complex the exercise, the higher the risk of injury and the lower the effectiveness.

Here's another debate for sports-specific training: resistance weight training versus functional training. I am disappointed in the health and fitness industry for over-promoting functional training and the resultant rise in popularity of the CrossFit style – constantly varied, high-intensity, functional movement. Certainly there are benefits, but the risk versus reward is high and it never gets better. Because of the complexity of using multiple muscle groups and joints during functional training, the law of diminishing return occurs early. You soon begin hitting your limits. Next, the complexities of the exercises cause you to lose form, resulting in a dramatic slowdown in improvement. To compensate, you add more weight, raising the chance of injury.

With the resistance weight training program I recommend, the law of diminishing return does apply, but safety is never compromised. Most likely, unless you are a professional athlete or competitive bodybuilder or powerlifter, you will never reach that point.

Gym Etiquette

Training is based on respect — for the equipment, the facility, the trainers and clients. Gym etiquette enables everyone to demonstrate that respect.

Equipment

1. All equipment must remain in the gym and cannot be removed for any reason. Outside equipment is not permitted.
2. Return weights and equipment to storage racks after each set. If someone is returning weights, wait until the weights are racked before you take your weights.
3. Do not place weights or equipment on the floor or benches between sets.
4. Be courteous and allow others access to weight equipment; do not monopolize.
5. If people are waiting, limit use of cardio machines to 30 minutes.
6. Use safety bars with the power rack.

Facility

1. All food and beverages are prohibited in the gym except for water in a plastic bottle.
2. Put all trash in provided containers. Keep the gym free of empty water bottles and papers.
3. Store outer clothing and other personal items in the provided lockers.

People

1. Be supportive and encouraging of others.
2. Respect the personal space and property of others.
3. Refrain from using foul or coarse language.
4. Turn off your cell phone while in the gym.

5. If you need a spotter for safety, ask for assistance after the person has finished their set.

6. Stay home if you are ill.

Getting Started with Your Workout Regimen

The first two weeks of your workout regimen will be different from the rest of your training. No matter what your level of fitness or your health and fitness goals when you first begin, it is important to ease into what will become your regular workout. Lifting weights is a skill and both your muscles and your nervous system need to be trained.

During the first two weeks you will be training your nervous system to instruct muscles and develop muscle memory. The best way to do this is to advance slowly and use repetition. Let me give you an example. If I read a series of ten telephone numbers and asked you to remember them all, you probably wouldn't be able to. But if I gave you one number, you would be able to remember it. If on the next day I asked you to repeat that number and gave you one more to memorize, you would be able to remember two numbers. If I continued for ten days — having you repeat the numbers previously memorized and adding one more each day, at the end of ten days you would be able to recite them all.

That's what you're asking your nervous system to do during the first weeks of training. As you build the neural groove that transmits instructions to the muscles, your muscles will remember the previous instructions and get better at following them. As your muscle memory improves, we'll gradually add more repetitions, increase the intensity of the workout with more weight, change the exercises, or a combination of all three.

So don't be discouraged if your initial two weeks don't seem as aggressive as you thought they would be. Follow the instructions, and you will soon progress to your regular workout routines.

Beginning Workout Regimen: 3 Days, Week 1

Day 1: Chest and Back

- Chest press incline: 3 sets x 10-12 reps (very light, no strain; keep track of weight)
- Lat pull down machine (back): 3 sets x 10-12 reps (very light, no strain; keep track of weight)
- Triceps push down: 3 sets x 10-12 reps (very light, no strain; keep track of weight)
- Biceps curl: 3 sets x 10-12 reps (very light, no strain; keep track of weight)

Day 2: Chest, Back and Legs

- Chest press incline: 3 sets x 10-12 reps (add a little more weight and/or reps; keep track of weight)
- Biangular lat pull down (back): 3 sets x 10-12 reps (add a little more weight and/or reps; keep track of weight)
- Triceps push down: 3 sets x 10-12 reps (add a little more weight and/or reps; keep track of weight)
- Biceps curl: 3 sets x 10-12 reps (add a little more weight and/or reps; keep track of weight)
- Leg press: 3 sets x 10-15 reps (very light, no strain; keep track of weight)

Day 3: Legs, Chest and Back

- Leg press: 4-5 sets x 15-20 reps (add a little more weight and/or reps; keep track of weight)
- Leg extension: 3 sets x 10 reps (very light, no strain; keep track of weight)
- Leg curls: 3 sets x 10 reps (very light, no strain; keep track of weight)
- Chest press incline: 3 sets x 10-15 reps (add a little more weight and/or reps; keep track of weight)

- Lat pull down machine (back): 3 sets x 10-12 reps (add a little more weight and/or reps; keep track of weight)

Beginning Workout Regimen: 3 Days, Week 2

Day 1: Chest and Back

- Chest press incline: 3 sets x 10-15 reps (add a little more weight and/or reps; keep track of weight)
- Lat pull down machine (back): 3 sets x 10-15 reps (add a little more weight and/or reps; keep track of weight)
- Low row (back): 3 sets x 10-15 reps (add a little more weight and/or reps; keep track of weight)
- Triceps push down: 3 sets x 10-15 reps (add a little more weight and/or reps; keep track of weight)
- Biceps curl: 3 sets x 10-15 reps (add a little more weight and/or reps; keep track of weight)

Day 2: Shoulders, Arms and Legs

- Shoulder press: 3 sets x 10-12 reps (very light, no strain; keep track of weight)
- Deltoid fly: 3 sets x 10-12 reps (very light, no strain; keep track of weight)
- Triceps push down: 3 sets x 10-12 reps (add a little more weight and/or reps; keep track of weight)
- Biceps curl: 3 sets x 10-12 reps (add a little more weight and/or reps; keep track of weight)
- Leg press: 3 sets x 10-15 reps (very light, no strain; keep track of weight)

Day 3: Legs

- Leg press: 5-7 sets x 15-30 reps (add a little more weight and/or reps; keep track of weight)

- Leg extension: 3 sets x 10-14 reps (add a little more weight and/or reps; keep track of weight)
- Leg curls: 3 sets x 10-15 reps (add a little more weight and/or reps; keep track of weight)

Now you should be ready to move to a regular program

Muscle Fatigue During Your Workout

Muscle adapts to stress (tension); the key is to continually change the level of stress. There is no need to make a change until you have reached the maximum adaptation at a particular stress level. Then you can change the level of stress by changing the exercise, changing the order of performing exercises on a muscle group, or changing the weight, number of reps or rest time. A good rule of thumb is to stay with an exercise program until you are not able to better a prior workout. When you are stagnant, it is time to change.

Partial muscle fatigue will occur during your workout. You can recognize one sign of muscle fatigue on the last rep, when it seems like you can't push or pull any more, but you don't give up or break proper form. You keep trying and the weight keeps moving but you get a slight tremor in the muscle and finish the rep totally fatigued. The tremor occurs because your brain is telling the muscle fibers that are not fully functional to start working. The fibers jump in and help out but since they do not have as much coordination as the other muscle fibers, they twitch. However, the next time you push the uncoordinated fibers, they will work much better with the rest of the fibers because of muscle memory (sometimes called *muscle groove*). Muscle memory and muscle groove are why you never forget how to ride a bicycle.

Muscle fatigue may occur when you are working as hard as you can without giving up or cheating on form but the weight is not moving. You stay with it and have someone give you a slight assist to start or finish the rep. This technique is a form of overtraining, so should be used with caution. However, it is useful to get you past a sticky spot since you are only as strong as your weakest link. By overtraining you strengthen the weak link and can return immediately to perfect form.

Another form of overtraining is using less-than-perfect form or slightly cheating (10-20%). I only recommend this for very advanced training. Drop sets – doing a set to failure then immediately reducing the weight and continuing with no rest – or doing multiple drop sets before taking a rest will also produce muscle fatigue.

Muscle fatigue is useful for your mental training. When you are working as hard as you can, using proper form, with a "can-do" attitude and not giving up, when you reach true muscle fatigue, you now know where your new max is to work on.

Rep, Rest and Training Techniques

Keep in mind that variety is the spice of life. To achieve the best overall health and fitness benefits, you'll need to change up reps and rest times. Here is a guide to help you determine the best reps and rest based on a specific goal.

- Low reps for maximum strength
  1-4 reps, with long rest (2+ minutes)
- Medium reps for general conditioning
  4-12 reps, rest 1-2 minutes
- High reps for muscular endurance
  12-25 reps, rest 1-2 minutes
- High reps for conditioning
  12-25 reps, rest 30 seconds – 1 minute
- Super high reps for muscular endurance
  25-100 reps, rest 1-3 minutes
- Super high reps for conditioning
  25-100 reps, rest 30 seconds-1 minute

Each set during the workout can be different. For example, on max chest day, once you establish a single rep max, lower the weight to the amount you think you can handle for 6-10 reps. For the next set, reduce the weight once again and aim for 12-20 reps.

I also like to train with low reps and plenty of rest for 2-3 weeks, then do the next workout with high reps (20-25) with a one minute rest. Or I will use 50% of my max weight and do 20 reps with a 30-second rest until I am unable to get more than 10 reps. (This usually takes 6-10 sets.)

Changing the rest between sets will make them harder or easier.

Here are some other training techniques:

- *Drop set.* Do as many reps as you can, then immediately lighten the weight and keep going. Do multiple drops before you rest. This is an overtraining technique to get past a sticky point, so be very selective when using this technique.
- *Giant set:* Do one exercise after the next for the same muscle group.
- *Super set:* Do one exercise after another of antagonistic muscle groups.
- *Pre-exhaustion set:* Exercise a muscle group just prior to the main muscle group. Example: chest flys before the bench press. Doing the flys fatigues the chest muscles while keeping the shoulders and triceps strong. This causes the shoulders and triceps to be less of a weak link in exercising the chest and makes the chest muscles work harder. Using a pre-exhaustion set is another form of overtraining to get past a sticky point, so again, be very selective when using this technique.
- *Forced reps:* A spotter helps you with reps that are impossible without assistance. I recommend limiting forced reps to 1 or 2 for the muscle group in a single workout. Forced reps are another form of overtraining to get past a sticky point, so again, be very selective when using this technique.

Muscle Soreness After Your Workout

The muscles used in resistance weight training are primarily the skeletal muscles. These muscles are attached to tendons and produce movement, maintain posture, stabilize joints and generate heat. Skeletal muscles work like a lever and have only two movements: contraction (shortening) or relaxing (lengthening). They are sometimes arranged in opposition so that when one muscle is contracting (shortening), the other is expanding (lengthening). The opposing muscles work in tandem to hold stagnant force, constant force (sustained work), and accelerating force (quick burst of power). The muscle fibers themselves are either fast twitch (stronger but having less endurance) or slow twitch (less strong but higher endurance) and are predominantly controlled by the somatic (voluntary) nervous system.

How muscles contract is a complicated topic, so let me give you an example using the rollup door at Fitness Results. Imagine you are using the chain to open the door. You face the chain, reach up with one arm, grab it and pull down. Then you reach up with your other arm, grab the chain and continue pulling down. You repeat this movement until the door is at the desired position. Now imagine you have thousands of arms working together to pull the chain. That is how muscle fibers work in the muscles.

Muscles need fuel to work, and that is provided when the body converts the carbohydrates and fat we eat into an energy source known as adenosine triphosphate (ATP). ATP is produced by one of two methods: aerobic (combining carbohydrates and fat with oxygen) and anaerobic (without oxygen). A byproduct of the anaerobic method is lactic acid, and its buildup in the muscle is what causes the burn you sometimes feel.

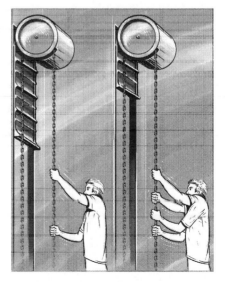

Opening the rollup door before and after a workout. That's how muscles work – more "arms" after the workout.

Let's put it all together! By performing resistance weight training with proper form, your muscle fibers learn to work together through the whole range of motion. Muscle coordination takes about two weeks to develop as the muscle fibers learn to perform together. After that, the muscle fibers begin to enlarge, producing more strength and coordination, muscle tone, muscle memory and a higher resting metabolic rate while continuing to add more muscle fibers, enhancing the process.

Muscle soreness that occurs during a workout is usually lactic acid buildup, while soreness after the workout is usually caused by inflammation of muscle fibers or damage from the stress of the workout. The soreness subsides as the inflammation goes down and the muscle fibers repair themselves. The best way to recover from this is to continue to use the muscle but at a significantly reduced stress level.

Over training – training too hard or too long – is a waste of time because it doesn't do your muscles any good. Too much stress causes so much damage that muscle fibers can't fully repair during the recovery time. Continuing to train anyway risks creating muscle scar tissue instead of building muscle fibers. The best practice is to train with proper form and full range of motion for a short time rather than overtraining of any kind.

Tips for an Effective Workout

A good, hard workout is doing the maximum amount of weight for the maximum amount of reps with endurance and perfect form — no cheating on form or giving up before muscle fatigue has truly set in. It could be heavy weight with low reps or light weight with lots of reps.

Hard work might mean working through your threshold for tolerating lactic acid buildup in your muscles. Hard work doesn't necessarily mean you're breathing hard and sweating, though that might be a byproduct of hard work.

Hard work means taking the proper amount of rest between sets. Rest allows your muscles to recover so you'll get the most out of the workout. Without adequate rest, the muscles won't have time to replenish with fuel and you'll invite premature failure from lack of fuel rather than muscle fatigue from hard work.

Secret #23: Hard work – doing the maximum amount of weight for the maximum amount of reps with endurance, perfect work, and adequate rest between sets – is what builds strength and muscle development.

The goal of every workout is to increase muscle strength, which occurs in two stages. First, the nerves in the muscle learn to work in a more coordinated manner, fire faster and recruit more muscle fibers to the task, leading to *muscle memory*. The second phase is actual enlargement of individual muscle fibers. It takes at least two weeks to develop muscle memory before muscle fibers begin to enlarge.

Sadly, it takes as little as one week without training to lose ground (though because of muscle memory, you don't drop back to the pre-training level). After even a short break from training, muscle fibers lose some of their strength and endurance and must be reconditioned. For this reason, it is best to minimize the breaks in training — especially at the beginning of your weight resistance training program — and to restart workout sessions at a lower level than before the break.

The more tension in the muscle at the beginning of the workout, the more force the muscle will have during the workout. To create tension without inducing too much fatigue, the workout starts with warm up sets of dynamic stretching, not static stretching. (If you want to static stretch, wait until after your workout and do static stretches.) A warm up set is very light — about 25% of the maximum weight — followed by two single rep sets of 50% and 80% of the max weight for this workout. The warm up is not fatiguing. Its purpose is to invoke muscle memory regarding the pathway of movement for the exercise, to be sure you can go through the entire range of motion without discomfort or impingement, to increase tension in the muscles, and to prepare you mentally for the increase in work and stress in the workout sets.

The amount of rest to take between sets is usually 1-2 minutes, though when you are working on a new personal best max weight goal, take as much time as you need without losing the heightened endorphin rush and tension you've built into your muscles. To increase conditioning, slightly shorten the rest time.

Bad training habits include not having a workout plan; moving from set to set with little rest; attempting too much weight so you can't maintain proper form; or doing lots of reps with bad form. It is not about the *quantity* of training, it is about the ***quality of the quantity*** of the training. Less is more when it comes to effective training. Using the Fitness Results training methods, you'll find that just three 30-minute sessions per week is enough to achieve your goals because you are training smarter and at a high intensity. You'll be surprised at how tiring a 30-minute workout can be. (As an aside, I have found that most men tend to over train with bad form, while most women do not push themselves hard enough.)

CHAPTER 6

About Training Methods

My training methods are based on resistance weight training, customized to reflect each client's personal fitness goals, physical ability and safety. Even though clients use the same equipment and perform the same training exercises, the actual training sessions will differ and continually change. This is the ultimate benefit of the 30-Minute Body training system – the training system is constantly assessing and adjusting so you get the maximum benefit.

If you have worked out at a gym or participated in athletics or read news accounts on health and fitness topics, you probably can name several different training methods. In addition, family and friends may tell you about training methods they are using or have heard about. Some of the best known are CrossFit, Pilates, P90X, TRX, Zumba, Les Mills, HIT (high intensity training), kick boxing, spinning, mixed martial arts, boot camp, circuit training, Tough Mudder.

As appealing as these training methods may sound, they may not be right for achieving your health and fitness goals. In fact, some may even work against them. For example, athletes use CrossFit to enhance their athletic performance. But for someone out of shape and just starting a fitness program, there is potential risk outweighing the potential benefits. Even for someone more advanced but not competing athletically, the complexity of CrossFit exercises raises the risk of injury while delivering minimum fitness benefits.

For someone who wants to add functional training but is not training for peak performance, suspension training like TRX is a safer option than CrossFit. However, since TRX requires coordination and core strength, it is not the best choice for beginners. In addition, beginners lack the ability to determine workload and capacity, making it hard to set goals and measure progress.

Many people consider Pilates to be a safe workout that improves flexibility and balance better than resistance weight training. In fact, suspension training like TRX is a better training method than Pilates. This is because with TRX, you are working against gravity. With Pilates you are working against springs. For a brief time, the new stress provided by the springs (or by resistance bands) will produce benefits. But over the long term, results from both Pilates and TRX will be far less when compared to resistance weight training.

In the last few years spinning has become very popular. While it is good for cardiovascular conditioning, spinning is not the best choice for weight loss because you could be decreasing muscle at a faster rate than you are decreasing fat.

My training methods emphasize resistance weight training because it is the best overall training method. Done correctly, resistance weight training is safe, has a low risk of injury, and produces steadily improving results. Other training methods are ancillary to resistance weight training. So stick to the basics – resistance weight training, proper nutrition and adequate rest – and add other training methods only after mastering resistance weight training. Occasional use of other training methods will add variety to your workout, as long as those methods are aligned with your goals and fitness level.

Why am I so convinced that resistance weight training is the best overall training method? Because over the years it has served me well personally, and because I have witnessed the results from doing over 100,000 personal training sessions with clients. From this experience I can say with confidence that resistance weight training is the safest, most effective and efficient means to achieve health and fitness goals. When performed properly and consistently over time, resistance weight training will help you maintain good health and fitness and fight the aging process. With any journey, there is more than one way to arrive at the destination. So even though resistance weight training is not the only way to maintain good health and fitness, I have seen for myself that it is the safest, most effective and most efficient way.

Weekly Resistance Weight Training Options

- **2 x week**
  - » Upper body (chest and back)
  - » Lower body (legs)

- **3 x week**
  - » Chest and back
  - » Legs
  - » Shoulders and arms

- **4 x week**
  - » Chest and biceps
  - » Legs (focus on quadriceps)
  - » Back and triceps
  - » Shoulders and arms (or hamstrings)

- **5 x week**
  - » Chest and biceps
  - » Legs (focus on quadriceps)
  - » Back and triceps
  - » Legs (focus on hamstrings)
  - » Shoulders and arms

Recommendations for Training Frequency

The optimum weekly frequency for training depends on your health and fitness goals, the time you are able to devote to training, your current fitness level and your age. If you make training a lifelong commitment, you may find that the optimum weekly frequency changes over time.

Two days of training a week is recommended for those with limited time to devote to training, or those recovering from injury. If your time is severely limited, it does no good to introduce unnecessary stress by committing to a more-frequency training schedule than you have time for.

Three days of training a week is optimum for most people. It provides a good balance between the time commitment and the results achieved. Training three times a week will double the benefit you'll get over two days per week.

Four days of training a week requires a significant time commitment. It is recommended for those whose training goals include peak performance. It is also good for seniors or others who may not be able to train as aggressively as needed for three days a week because of age or injury limitations.

Five days of training a week is a serious commitment of time and effort and is generally used by professional athletes or for a specific performance goal. Conversely, it may also be good for individuals who prefer to work out more frequently so they don't have to exert as much stress as they would for less-frequent training sessions.

Whatever your initial training frequency, be flexible. Adjust the frequency either temporarily or permanently to account for changes in your health and fitness goals.

Example Workout: 2 days per week

Training two days a week focuses on the upper body (chest, back and arms) and lower body (legs).

Day 1: Chest, back, rear deltoids and arms

Bench press or incline dumbbell press	1 warmup + 3 sets x 8-12 reps
Chest fly	2 sets x 10-15 reps
Lat pull down	1 warmup + 3 sets x 8-12reps
Low row	3 sets x 10-15 reps
Mid row	3 sets x 10-15 reps
Deltoid fly	1 warmup + 3 sets x 10-15 reps
Triceps	1 warmup + 3 sets x 10-20 reps
Biceps curl	1 warmup + 3 sets x 10-20 reps

Day 2: Legs

Squat, leg press or hack squat	3-5 sets x 5-10 reps
Leg extension	3 sets x 8-15 reps
Hamstring curls	3 sets x 8-15 reps

For more workout examples go to www.FitnessResults.com

Example Workout: 3 days per week

Training three days a week includes lower body (legs), provides more variety for chest and back exercises, and adds shoulder and arm exercises.

Day 1: Chest and back

Bench press	1 warm up + 3 sets x 8-12 reps
Chest press incline	1-2 sets x 8-15 reps
Chests fly	3 sets x 10-15 reps
Lat pull down	1 warmup + 3 sets x 3-15 reps
Low row	3 sets x 10-15 reps
Mid row	3 sets x 10-15 reps

Day 2: Legs

Squat, leg press or hack squat	5-8 sets x 10-35 reps
Leg extension	3 sets x 8-15 reps
Hamstring curls	3 sets x 8-15 reps

Day 3: Shoulders, biceps, triceps

Shoulder press	1 warm up + 3 sets x 4-15 reps
Deltoid fly	3 sets x 10-15 reps
Triceps	1 warm up + 3 sets x 4-15 reps
Biceps curl	1 warm up + 3 sets x 4-15 reps

For more workout examples go to www.FitnessResults.com

Example Workout: 4 days per week

Day 1: Chest and biceps

Bench press	1 warm up + 3 sets x 1-20 reps
Incline dumbbell press	1-2 sets x 8-12 reps
Dumbbell fly	1-2 sets x 10-15 reps
Alternating dumbbell curl	1 warm up + 3 sets x 6-15 reps

Day 2: Legs

Squat, leg press or hack squat	6-10 sets x 1-20 reps
Leg extension	3 sets x 8-15 reps
Hamstring curls	3 sets x 8-15 reps

Day 3: Back and triceps

Lat pull down	1 warmup + 4 sets x 3-20 reps
Low row	3 sets x 8-15 reps
High row	3 sets x 8-15 reps
Triceps	1 warm up + 3 sets x 10-15 reps

Day 4: Shoulders and arms

Shoulder press	1 warm up + 3 sets x 4-15 reps
Deltoid fly	3 sets x 10-15 reps
Triceps	1 warm up + 3 sets x 4-15 reps
Biceps curl	1 warm up + 3 sets x 4-15 reps

For more workout examples go to www.FitnessResults.com

Example Workout: 5 days per week

Five workouts a week provides more aggressive training (more sets, more reps) and has more variety of exercises.

Day 1: Chest and biceps

Bench press	1 warm up + 3 sets x 1-20 reps
Incline dumbbell press	1-2 sets x 8-12 reps
Dumbbell fly	1-2 sets x 10-15 reps
Biceps curl	1 warm up + 3 sets x 6-15 reps

Day 2: Legs

Squat, leg press or hack squat	6-10 sets x 1-20 reps
Leg extension	3 sets x 8-15 reps

Day 3: Back, biceps, triceps

Lat pull down	1 warmup + 4 sets x 3-20 reps
Low row	3 sets x 8-15 reps
High row	3 sets x 8-15 reps
Triceps	1 warm up + 3 sets x 10-15 reps

Day 4: Shoulders and arms

Shoulder press	1 warm up + 3 sets x 4-15 reps
Deltoid fly	3 sets x 10-15 reps
Triceps	1 warm up + 3 sets x 4-15 reps
Biceps curl	1 warm up + 3 sets x 4-15 reps

Day 5: Hamstrings

Deadlift	4-6 sets x 1-10 reps
Hamstring curl	3-4 sets x 10-15 reps

For more workout examples go to www.FitnessResults.com

CHAPTER 7

My Personal Workout and Gym Experience

After I stopped competing, I didn't stop training. In fact, I still train today which has made me very strong for my age. For example, I have a 24-year-old client who was drafted as a defensive tackle with the Pittsburgh Steelers football team. I am still strong enough to motivate him to push to new maxes when we train together. But I've reached the declining years of my strength, so sometimes I feel weak compared to what I was able to do just a few years ago. I've accepted that I will never again have the strength resulting from the work, dedication, time commitment, stress and constant aches and pains brought on by training for peak performance. I like the idea of being strong but at my age I lack the capacity to work out at the level I managed when I was training to compete.

Sometimes it is hard for me even to recall what it took to achieve and maintain that level of fitness training. It has become remote, like when I hear a discussion of the national debt or the national budget spending. It sounds like a lot, but I can't really quite grasp what it means. Today I'm very happy to be in good physical condition and to work out at a level that is comfortable and produces minimal injuries and discomfort. For the most part, I feel great with high energy and no stress.

And yes, it is a challenge for me to continue training, just like it is for everyone else. My goal is four workouts a week. Sometimes I don't make the time for all four and settle for two in a week. When this happens, I notice a real decline in my strength and endurance. Recently I re-committed to four workouts a week without sacrificing my sleep. That takes determination but the payback is huge. I believe it is the single most important thing you can do for yourself, and the closest thing you'll ever find to the mythical fountain of youth. I'm a hands-on business owner with employees to manage and a weekly workload of 80 personal training appointments a week, which makes it a challenge to always get in four weekly workouts. But if I do this consistently, it makes the rest of my day a lot easier and productive.

My First Gym Experience

I joined my first gym in 1977. It was a local gym called R&R Bodybuilding. Back then, gyms were a lot different than now. Guys and girls didn't work out together. Smaller gyms like R&R were all male, and the women's gym in our area was called the Ladies Spa. One larger gym, Jack La Lanne's, was co-ed but with a twist: Monday, Wednesday and Friday were reserved for men and Tuesday, Thursday and Saturday for women. Another large chain gym opened as co-ed but split the building in two with a gym on one side for guys and on the other side for girls.

Another big difference between then and now is that it was legal to use steroids. At R&R, steroid use was prevalent, as was *'roid rage* – fights that broke out almost daily. A common fight subject was what music was playing in the gym but there were lots of other topics that started fights. Free weights were scattered all over the floor, and a lot of serious weight lifting was being done.

The gym was largely unsupervised. The only employee was the manager,

Tony, who wanted to be a bodybuilder. His dad was a successful businessman who opened the gym for Tony. It was located in a strip mall and maybe 1700 square feet in all. Tony would open the gym, work out, then ask whoever was in the gym to watch the place for an hour while he ran errands, then leave for the rest of the day, returning only to lock up. The guy who was training would finish his workout and ask the next guy to watch the gym. That's how it went nearly every day. Sometimes when you showed up to work out, guys would be on the roof getting a tan before their next bodybuilding competition. I have fond memories of that gym – my first true love (LOL).

Since this was my first gym experience and I was learning how to work out, I looked for guidance to the other guys in the gym. I noticed that the more serious guys varied the body parts they trained, depending on the day. By paying attention and asking question, I came to understand the strategy behind that technique.

Following that technique, I originally did upper body one day and lower body the next – a 2-day cycle repeated continuously, seven days a week. I was in great condition but without knowing it, was overtraining and not seeing much improvement. I had reached the point of diminishing return.

As I learned more, I switched to a 3-day cycle of chest, triceps, biceps, shoulders, forearms and abs on Day 1; legs, calves and abs on Day 2; and back, biceps, triceps, forearms and abs on Day 3, still repeated continuously, seven days a week. After I made the switch from a 2-day to a 3-day cycle, I began to improve.

About two years after I joined R&R Bodybuilding, it was sold to three guys, all named Paul. They changed the name to Fitness Connection and began running it in a more businesslike manner. They established rules for the gym, hired a front counter person to always be present, and brought in some new equipment. There were way fewer fights, weights were put away instead of being left on the floor and the work out environment improved. I continued to train 7 days a week and spent as much time as possible at the gym. I was always trying different things to see what would make a difference. There was a lot of trial-and-error back then.

Next the three Pauls decided to let girls work out with the guys. At first they had assumed women would not want to train with guys, but they figured it wouldn't hurt to make the gym co-ed. Several girls joined the gym and with girls came more guys. Shortly after, more gyms became co-ed, slowly evolving to where we are today.

I remember two very attractive girls who joined Fitness Connection and worked out together. They were very friendly and always in good spirits. They asked if they could work out with me and some of the other guys, and I always said yes. When they showed up to work out, guys would come out of the woodwork and the gym would be packed. As soon as the girls finished their workout, the gym would empty. It never failed – the girls showed up and the gym would be packed. I don't know how the guys knew when the girls would be there, but they always did.

I Begin to Understand Muscle Training

I was in high school when I joined R&R Bodybuilding. When I started working full time, a lot changed. It was much more challenging to get my workouts in, so I joined several gyms simultaneously. One opened earlier and one stayed open later; one had a piece of equipment I wanted to use. I decided what gyms to join based on my need at the time. (I also remember those days because there was no air conditioning in the gyms and smog was really bad in the area at the time. Thank goodness California has made such great improvements in air quality!)

Remembering the instant improvement when I changed from a 2-day program cycle to 3-day, I started thinking about my overall program. I realized I was making some mistakes that were holding me back. For instance, why was I doing triceps after chest and biceps and back? When you train the chest, you are also working shoulders and triceps. The primary muscle group is chest, but the secondary group is shoulders and triceps. Similarly, when training the back you also train biceps and shoulders. So the program I was using wasn't logical.

Even though I hadn't completely figured out the best way to train my shoulders, I tried changing to chest and biceps. I realized that my triceps were already fully trained and by including them after chest, not only was I overtraining them, I was not able to train them to their full potential. The same thing applied to my biceps. After I made the change, I noticed improvement. Even though I was training biceps and triceps after a big muscle group (chest and back), I was able to train them to their full potential.

These results made me really think about muscle groups – primary, secondary and so on. Knowing I would be working out 7 days a week, I designed my program accordingly. By now I was about 23 years old and had explored all kinds of training regimens – circuit training, high reps, low reps, low rest, high rest (which was very common at the time). And even though it was mostly guys working out in the gym with a lot of guy talk and messing around, we got a lot of good workouts then.

I mention this because it is the time I began to understand what makes a proper workout program. I still had much to learn (in fact, to this day I am still learning). When I notice "fitness experts" on Instagram or other social media who look good and are dispensing fitness advice with only two of three years of experience, I'm taken aback. When I started, I trained 7 days a week with some of the best and it still took 9 years before I felt I understood body mechanics well enough to devise an effective workout program.

Here's the first really effective program I developed, rotating 7 days a week:

- Day 1: Chest, biceps
- Day 2: Quadriceps and calves
- Day 3: Back, traps and triceps
- Day 4: Shoulders, arms, biceps and triceps with higher reps, forearms
- Day 5: Hamstrings and calves

What was different about this program is I did less abs because I noticed I was getting a thick, muscled core from heavy squatting, meaning it was a waste of time for me to work them regularly. With this program I was seeing even better results.

Then I noticed that my front deltoids were overdeveloped compared to the rear delts. Without realizing it, I had created a muscle imbalance with work on the bench press and incline press. So I stopped doing anything specific to train the front delts. I continue to struggle with balance between my front and rear delts. Even when I stopped training my front delts, they still overpowered my rear delts.

An Experiment with Calf Muscles and Forearms

I was not seeing growth in my calf muscles, so I devised a challenging experiment. I dedicated more than 30 minutes a day just to my calf muscles, varying between heavy weight and high reps, always with great form, control and full range of motion. The workouts were brutal. On a heavy weight day, I would max out the machine weight at 1000 lbs. and do a standing calf raise. That's a short range of motion with a very strong muscle group. For the seated calf raise, I would go over 400 lbs. On high rep days, I would do well over 100 reps. Sometimes I would train by time – 1 or 2 minutes. My calf muscles grew fantastically. But then I noticed a lot of joint pain in my ankles, knees, hips, back and shoulders. After several weeks of daily training, I decreased to two days on, one day off to give my body a rest. I finally stopped altogether to avoid injury.

While I was training my calf muscles, I was working on forearms with the same intensity of training. I noticed the same type of discomfort from the excessive workouts, so stopped that, too. I asked myself why I was doing all that work on calves and forearms when it wasn't contributing to my overall strength. If I had been a bodybuilder (I wasn't), I would only work these muscle groups a few months before a competition.

This turned out to be invaluable knowledge. To develop a muscle, you have to stress it beyond what it is used to. In daily life, calf muscles are stressed with every step we take. My training had indeed caused more stress than my calf muscles were used to, and by training them every day, I was constantly increasing the stress. My calf muscles grew by 3 inches in just a few weeks but the excessive training had also increased the risk of injury. Now when a client wants to develop the calf muscle, I know how it can be done and I am also able to explain the risk so the client can make an informed decision.

The same logic applies to other muscle groups, such as abs, core and traps, that are used in daily life. Secondary or supporting muscle groups will automatically be trained with their corresponding primary muscles. Knowing this means you can stop wasting time and energy on training that isn't needed, and focus on training the muscles that will provide the best results.

The Benefit of Training Partners

Even people like me who have plenty of internal motivation can benefit from having a training partner. My brother Daren has often been my partner over the years. Both he and I are adopted, so we don't have the same natural strength. But the longer we trained together, the stronger he got. He could have been a competitive powerlifter but never had the desire. Nevertheless, he was always there to help me. He also had a bad motorcycle accident, suffering two broken femurs, a punctured lung and a lot of other injuries. He is lucky to be alive. He now has rods in both legs and for a time, no one knew if he would walk again or if he would have a bad limp.

Daren was in the hospital for months. When he finally got home, I started working with him, first with a walker, then crutches, then in the gym. He was called to begin physical therapy, and when he walked into the therapist's office with only a slight limp, the therapist was amazed. Upon learning that Daren had been training with me at the gym, the therapist declared Daren should keep on training and skip physical therapy. He did. Today, not only does Daren no longer have a limp, he completed the police academy, graduating at the top of his class.

Over the years, I've worked out a lot with my good friend Ron Graciano. Ron's strength is different than mine. He is not as strong as I am at peak strength, but he can do multiple sets at his peak weight. Sometimes he is even better on his second set, while I have to reduce the weight on each consecutive set. What accounts for the difference is the type of muscle fiber. Slow twitch muscle fibers have less pure strength but better endurance, while fast twitch muscle fibers provide quick bursts of energy.

Ron's slow twitch fibers made him well suited to endurance sports like running and cycling. But Ron became a bodybuilder by training with both heavy weight/low reps and low weight/high reps for multiple sets. His slow twitch fibers made him able to train with very heavy weight for reps with an incredible recovery rate between sets.

My fast twitch fibers were natural for powerlifting. But I also conditioned my slow twitch fibers. I once bench pressed 315 lbs. for 68 reps and was just starting to tire. I'm not sure how many more I could have done, but at least several more. I am not considered an endurance guy, but 68 reps at 315 lbs. is an example of great endurance.

How I Achieved Peak Performance

On the bench press, my best performance was 23 reps at 405 lbs., 11 reps at 495 lbs., and 1 rep at 605 lbs. This was not a level of stress I could maintain for longer periods. Usually I would peak, then subside. My average performance was 10-15 reps at 405 lbs. and 1-6 reps at 495 lbs. I rarely did 315 lbs. for reps. Instead I would use a narrow grip, keeping my elbows close to my body and forearms over my elbows. The narrow grip puts more emphasis on the triceps (my weakest link) than on my shoulders, as I usually had a problem locking out at the top.

The pectoral or chest muscles will never be the weakest link in the bench press. Usually it will be either triceps or shoulders. Here's how to tell which is the weakest link. If you have a hard time locking out the arms, the weak link is triceps. If you can lift the bar 3-5 inches off your chest, probably both your shoulders and triceps that need work. If you can't get the weight off your chest, it is your shoulders (though the triceps could also be lacking).

To work the triceps, narrow your grip, keep the elbows close to the body, and always keep the forearms over the elbows. My strong grip is my ring finger on the groove of the bar. If I want to force my triceps to work harder, I move my grip in so my middle finger is on the grove, or maybe even closer. Then when I lower the bar to my chest, it will be 1-2 inches lower or further away from my chin. My elbows will be slightly closer to my body, and the bar will be over my elbows. The closer your hands, the lower the bar, and the closer the elbows are to the body. Your grip should never be narrower than your shoulders. To get an idea of how to do a proper bench press close grip, try doing a reverse grip bench press. The exercises have the same purpose, though a reverse grip puts more stress on the wrist.

I also like the incline chest press as a chest exercise. It offers a greater range of motion than the bench press and puts more emphasis on the front deltoids. You will usually use less weight on the incline than with the bench press. I do recommend varying the angle of the bench occasionally, between 30 degrees and 45 degrees.

For incline press, I've always preferred dumbbells over the bar. For me, the bar impedes movement and keeps me in an uncomfortable range of motion. I have worked through that discomfort and achieved acceptable performance at incline press: 455 lbs. – not great, but not bad. I once had a set of 200 lb. dumbbells that I used to do 15 reps on incline press.

Shoulder press is the same; I prefer dumbbells to the bar. My best bar shoulder press was 405 lbs. for 4 reps. I could do the 200 lb. dumbbell for 10 reps. Technically, the dumbbell should be harder but sometimes if one exercise feels better than a comparable one, you might be stronger on the more difficult one that is more comfortable for you.

For a long time I did bench press and incline press in the same workout. I stopped that a few years ago when I realized it is overtraining the chest. Occasionally I will do one less set on the bench press and no more than two sets on the incline press. But I prefer two weeks of bench press and one week of dumbbell press.

I finish my chest workout with 2 sets of flys. Chest flys should not be used as a heavy exercise to build muscle; the press exercises achieve that.

The chest fly with a moderate weight is a nice finisher. Even in the years I was competing, I never used more than 55 lb. dumbbells and now I never use more than 35 lbs. At one time I did chest flys with 140 lb. dumbbells. Over time I overstretched the muscles and began having pain in my sternum. It took me months to get better.

My back has always been strong. Even with a body weight of 280 lbs, I could do 20 pullups with one 200 lb. dumbbell hanging off me to increase my body weight. (I attached the dumbbell to a chain which was attached to a weight belt.) I never tried to see how many pullups I could do without the added weight, but I know it would have been a lot.

I stopped doing T-bar rows and bent-over rows long ago to avoid injury. While I was still doing them, I knew that unsupported exercises were more risky, but figures the rewards were worth it. I was completely wrong. I had a very bad back injury that kept me from training for over a week, and took several more weeks to completely heal. After that I began training my back with supported exercises and my back has gotten even stronger. I realize now it is never worth the risk to do unsafe exercises.

While I was competing, I had a piece of old Nautilus leverage equipment that I loved. I could use it to do low rows, high rows and shrugs. I could load it to 1100 lbs. When I stopped competing, I got rid of it and a lot of other great pieces of equipment to save space and use time more efficiently with my personal training clients. Now I use mainly selectorized strength equipment (*i.e.,* equipment with a stack of weight plates and a weight selection key) that is good for my clients and me, as I no longer train with extremely heavy weights.

Secret #24: With proper form, a workout is one of the safest things you will do all day.

Even if you are using a weight that seems very heavy, it doesn't compare to the stress resulting from impact. Stepping off a curb or going down a stairway can put much more stress on your body than moving 400 lbs. in a leg press.

Strange as it seems, picking up a dropped pencil may cause more injury than lifting a heavy weight. When you bend over to pick up a pencil, you aren't thinking about using proper form. You might bend sideways at the waist, rounding your back, keeping your legs straight and knees locked while you stretch to reach the pencil. Now you are susceptible to herniating a disc. Conversely, when preparing to lift a heavy weight, we think about it and use proper form. When lifting with proper form, there is very little risk of injury.

Learn From My Mistake

I have not kept my back as strong as my chest because of injuries. One day I was hooking my large boat and trailer to my truck. I backed the truck up to the trailer hitch, got out of the truck, and walked back to the hitch, only to discover that the truck and boat were just a few inches apart. I know what I should have done was to get back in the truck and move it those extra few inches. That would have been smart. But that's not what I did. Instead, I made one of my biggest mistakes. I grabbed the trailer with my right arm and pulled it to the truck. I heard and felt my muscle tear. I knew right away this was not good. Luckily, it was not a complete tear, just a fairly bad partial tear of the tendon. Also luckily, the trailer hitch was over the truck and I was able to hook them up without moving the truck.

What I don't know is whether the tear would have happened anyway. The tendon might have been getting weaker and was going to tear eventually; I just made it happen sooner. It might have been healthy and strong and it tore because I overstressed it. Or I could have had a muscle imbalance which over time would have caused the tear. I'll never know. But for the record, I did overstress the muscle.

I mention this because when a client wakes up with a pain or problem, they inevitably want to blame the workout, even if it was days earlier. If you train properly, even with a weight that is heavy for you, it is one of the safest things you will do all day.

My next mistake was not going to the doctor right away to have the tear checked out. I'm not sure if a doctor could have done anything to help the tendon, but I should have gone to find out. I did not, and it affected not only my biceps strength, but my back strength, as you are only as strong as your weakest muscle. After a few weeks, I started doing rehab on the bicep. I started with 5 lb. dumbbell for 10 reps. It was very painful and tiring. My brain was protecting the injury, so did not want to do the work. It took a huge amount of concentration to do just one rep. Nevertheless, I continued to use the 5 lb. dumbbell every day and after a few days I was able to move up to the next weight. This continued for several months. When I reached 30-35 lbs. of weight with the dumbbells, I switched from daily to just a few days a week.

While I was rehabbing, I was able to work most of my muscle groups, except back and biceps. My bicep was swollen for over a year. After a year I had regained acceptable strength, though not as much as before the injury. Before the injury I could do one-arm preacher curls with a 120 lb. dumbbell for 10 reps, and EZ-bar curls with 255 lbs. for 15 reps with good form. After the injury, the best I could do was 70 lb. dumbbells for 10 reps – not even close to my condition before the injury. Prior to the injury I could do drop sets of 10 reps with the 120 lbs. dumbbells and immediately switch to the 110 lbs. dumbbells for 10 reps. I would keep dropping 10 lbs. each set of 10 reps, and finally stop at the 50 lbs. dumbbells.

More bad news. Just as I was getting some of my strength back, I suffered another tear. I was doing one-arm preacher dumbbell curls. On my fourth set of 15 reps, *déjà vu*. I heard the tearing sound and felt the tear, this time in my other bicep. It wasn't as bad as the first tear, but still bad enough. This illustrates what I mentioned previously: if it's going to happen, it's going to happen. I had warmed up, the weight was not heavy, it was a light day with more reps, and of course it happened on the last rep of my last set. Luckily the rehab was faster than before but I lost strength that I will never get back. Now I can only do 6 pullups with no additional weight before my arms begin hurting too bad to continue.

Legs

Let's discuss everyone's favorite exercise day: legs! For me, leg day was a love/hate relationship. I loved the challenge and even loved the work, to a point. But to work my legs to their full potential took me to a whole new level.

In the beginning I did the standard workout: 3-4 sets of my main leg exercise (leg press, squats or something comparable) then 3 sets of leg extensions and curls. I thought I was getting a good workout. Then I realized that we stand and walk a lot during the day. This means we are stressing the leg muscles, so we have to work legs a lot harder than other muscle groups to stress them into better performance. I started doing more sets of my primary leg exercise and less sets of some upper body muscle groups. I found I could not go straight to the volume I wanted, so each workout I tried to do a little more. As my strength, endurance and tolerance grew, I was able to do more.

I constantly pushed. Over time I was doing a tremendous amount of volume. That's when I discovered that the legs themselves are not the weakest link in moving forward. Your mind or your desire to work harder will keep you back. I found that if I worked hard in the beginning with higher reps and without worrying about conserving my strength and energy, I could actually lift more. By raising reps on beginning sets – *i.e.,* focusing more on reps than lbs. – you increase muscle tension, raise your tolerance level, and have the confidence you need to move to the next weight. If you complete 10 reps at one weight level, you know that you can get the next small increase. Here is what my average leg day training was after I learned this:

First exercise squats

- Set 1: 135 lbs. x 10 reps
- Set 2: 225 lbs. x 10 reps
- Set 3: 315 lbs. x 10 reps
- Set 4: 405 lbs. x 10 reps
- Set 5: 495 lbs. x 10 reps
- Set 6: 585 lbs. x 6 reps

- Set 7: 635 lbs. x 4 reps
- Set 8: 675 lbs. x 4 reps

I might stop at 8 sets or continue for a few more sets, depending on my training cycle. Then I would do 10 more sets of 10 reps with between 495-585 lbs. depending on my training program, followed by 3 sets of 10-15 reps of leg extensions. The workouts were crazy and grueling, but very effective.

Then out of nowhere I had a real problem with my squat. After I lowered to the bottom of the squat movement and started to rise back to the starting position, I came up way too fast at the hips which meant my shoulders didn't stay over my hips. That left my back bent too far forward, causing me to use too much back muscle to get the weight up. I did get the weight back up to rack it but I had really hurt my back. This was the beginning of the end of my squats. I started rehabbing my back with a *reverse hyper* machine.

The first working reverse hyper machine was created by Louie Simmons. Its goal is to provide pulling forces (traction) along the spine to decompress the disc. Powerlifters like it because the decompression helps reverse the compression on the spine after heavy squatting. The machine

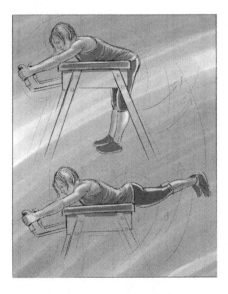

is a raised platform. You lie on it with your hips at the end of the platform and legs hanging down toward the floor. Your ankles go between two rollers attached to a weight. With legs straight, you raise your legs as far as you can, aiming to get your ankles as high as your hips by engaging your lats, butt and hamstrings without arching your lower back. Slowly lower your legs and repeat the movement. The weight should be light enough for you to do 10 reps while maintaining perfect form.

Reverse hyper rehab exercise

I started doing the reverse hyper

exercises with 3 sets of 20 reps with no weight. I did these every day for the first week then every other day. As the weight got heavier, I did the exercise less often until I reached once a week. Soon I was doing pretty good weight. I could do 3 sets of 20 reps with 3 x 45 lb. plates on each side and my back was as strong as ever.

After I was able to return to squats, my shoulders began to hurt. I visited my doctor who sent me for an MRI test of shoulders and neck. Then I returned to the doctor to review the test results. When he saw me in the waiting room, he stopped abruptly and said, "Mr. McCullough, come with me!" He seemed agitated as he opened the door to the hallway. He was walking ahead of me, talking all the while. "Your shoulder is fine but your neck is ruined," he said. He didn't stop talking as we entered the examining room. Again he said, "Your neck is ruined. You have to stop working out. You are too young for surgery." I was very nervous, thinking, *what is he talking about?"* The doctor finally calmed down and explained that because of the heavy lifting I had done, I had arthritis. From the heavy squats, I had calcification and the beginning of nerve damage. If I kept up with heavy lifting, I would need surgery and would never lift again. But if I moved to lighter workouts and stopped squatting, I would be able to keep the condition from worsening.

I took the doctor's advice. I stopped doing squats and heavy overhead and incline presses. Since I made those changes, my condition has not worsened. But it did cause me to make huge changes in my leg routine. I changed from heavy weights to high reps on the leg press. The first time with this change, I put 1 x 45 lbs. on each side of the leg press and did 100 reps. The next set I added 1 x 45 lbs. to each side and did as many consecutive reps as I could without stopping. I think I hit 60 before I took a brief rest at the top of the movement then finished the set. The next set I added another 1 x 45 lbs. for as many reps as I could. For each subsequent set, I added another 45 lbs. for as many reps as I could. The reps kept dropping and when they got to 20, I could get 20 for the rest of my sets. The leg press holds 11 x 45 lbs. plates per side, so I did 11 sets on the leg press then finished with 3 sets on the leg extension.

The next leg workout, I repeated the routine but made sure to better it over the previous workout. 100 reps was still my goal, without stopping for rest during the set. I was able to better each workout until I was getting 100 consecutive reps for all 11 sets.

To make it harder, I began doing super sets with the leg extension and leg press. I warmed up on the leg extension with 15 reps, then worked up to doing the stack, followed by 11 x 45 lbs. x 2 on the leg press for 100 reps continuously for 10 sets. With this routine, I did not lose any muscle in my legs from not being able to do heavy squats.

I was looking for a new leg challenge and thought I had given my neck enough of a rest. I returned to doing squats but on equipment with shoulder pads, like a hack squat. I also used a Paramount total leg machine and a Magnum perfect squat. Everything was going well until I had a bad accident on my

mountain bike. I fractured my back and now have permanent nerve damage that affects my feet and legs. I have learned to deal with it and am able to work my legs pretty well, though not nearly what I was able to do before. But it is enough to keep strength and conditioning.

This may sound worse than it is. I can do as much weight during leg exercises as the 24-year-old client that was just drafted by the Pittsburgh Steelers football team, and he is extremely strong. But if I keep training him and he continues to get stronger, I am not sure I will be able to keep up.

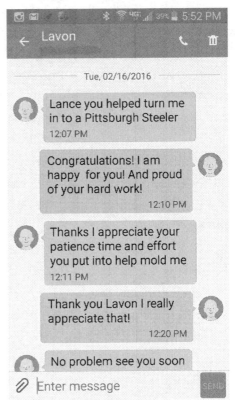

Lavon: 24 year old Pittsburgh Steeler Draftee

Quads and Hamstrings

Exercising legs meant working one day on quadriceps and another day on hamstrings. I split the muscles into two days for the same reason I split chest and back. If you are training your quads hard, you won't be able to work your hamstrings properly. Also, any time you are working the quads, you will have some involvement from hamstrings and vice versa.

I have always had a strong deadlift which I attribute to having a strong core and to working on squats. My weakest link in deadlift was my grip. I couldn't hold more than 900 lbs. without straps even though I could do 765 lbs. for more than 10 reps for 3 sets. I relied on doing different types of leg curls to build hamstring strength, concentrating on good form by keeping my back and glutes uninvolved. I also changed my foot position on the leg press by putting my feet high on the foot plate of the leg press to increase the emphasis on my hamstrings.

Secret #25: When working your legs, they will not be the weakest link. Your mind, desire and tolerance will be the limiting factor.

Even at my peak performance, I always knew I could do more. For legs, I like to "pyramid up" with working warmup sets. If I decided to establish a new single-rep max, I would do a warmup set, then continue with more weight and high reps. As the weight increased, I would gradually reduce the reps a little on each successive set as needed and continue to build muscle tension.

This is an entirely different strategy than working the chest, where after the warm up set, you do single reps as you add weight. With the chest, the fatigue factor will overcome the tension factor; with legs, the fatigue factor will not overtake the tension factor. By training legs with higher reps as weight increases, we increase muscle tension and mentally build confidence.

Here's how it works: I complete 10 reps at a set weight, then increase the weight. Knowing that I just completed 10 reps at the lower weight, I am confident I will be able to do some reps at the new weight (perhaps 8). Now I increase the weight again, still confident that I can complete some reps. Keep repeating the cycle of max reps at one weight, then increasing it until you reach the single-rep max weight. Using this method, I will achieve a much higher weight level than I ever thought possible.

Let's contrast that with the usual method of achieving a single-rep max. Beginning with a set weight, do a single rep, which does not build much muscle tension. Now increase the weight and do another rep. If this is a struggle, how much confidence will you have that you can increase the weight and still complete reps?

I have a technique that shows clients the power of the mind and demonstrates the effectiveness of my method. First I use single reps with each weight increase until the client reaches the point where they cannot achieve a single rep. Then I reduce the weight and have the client do as many reps as possible. This time when I begin adding weight, I have the client do max reps at that weight. Several sets later, we'll be past the weight where they failed earlier and the client often can complete 10 or more reps.

I Change My Training Style

In 1995, I suffered a lot of injuries, and that affected my training progress. I had been thinking about trying a totally different style of training, and in early 1996 I made the change.

The system was complex. Saturday and Sunday were heavy training days, mimicking a competition. Then on competition day, it would feel like a training day rather than competition. Monday, Tuesday and Wednesday were high rep days. Thursday and Friday were for percentage and speed training.

Both my training styles had pros and cons. My old style was great at building strength, except it meant too many injuries, causing me to lose strength and conditioning. The new system was great at building strength and kept me free from injury from 1996-1999, which were my most competitive years.

The negative of the new system was its complexity and the fact that if I missed just one workout, it would set me back weeks. It was very stressful.

Here's how complex the schedule was:

(Left): 1998 AAU National Bench Press championship medal. (Right): Lance (visible in background between the spotters) performing bench press during 1998 AAU National Championship. Photo demonstrates why power lifting is not a popular spectator sport.

- **Saturday:** upper body max day. 1 rep max as the primary exercise; 80-90% of max for reps as the secondary exercise. Repeating on a four-week cycle.
  - » *Week 1:* bench press (strong or wide grip), 1 rep max; lat pull down 1-3 rep max; upper back row 4-8 reps, 2 sets.
  - » *Week 2*: incline press 1 rep max; close-grip bench press, 3-5 reps, 2 sets; low row 2 rep max; deltoid fly 6-10 rep max, 2 sets.
  - » *Week 3*: shoulder press, 1 rep max; flat dumbbell press (palms facing in, elbows close to body), 3-5 max rep, 2 sets; upper back row, 2 rep max; lat pulldown (different grip from week 4), 4-8 rep max, 2 sets.
  - » *Week 4*: close-grip bench press, 1 rep max; shoulder press 3-5 reps, 2 sets
- **Sunday:** squats and dead lifts, max day, in a 3-4 week repeating cycle:
  - » *Week 1:* squats, working up to a single rep max; dead lift, working up to a 1 rep max.
  - » *Week 2:* front squat, 4 rep max, 3 sets
  - » *Week 3:* box squat (low box), 3 rep max, 3 sets; partial dead lift (bar is raised a few inches above the ground with blocks), 3 reps, 3 sets.
  - » *Week 4:* hack squats, 2 rep max, 3 sets.

- **Monday:** all exercises with 1 minute or less rest between sets; using either time or reps; usually less than 50% of 1 rep max
  - » Dumbbell shoulder press, 2 sets to failure
  - » Rear deltoids, 2 sets
  - » Biceps exercise different from previous Thursday, 2 sets to failure
  - » Core exercise, 2 sets
  - » Reverse hyper, 2 sets
- **Tuesday:** all exercises with 1 minute or less rest between sets; using either time or reps; usually less than 50% of 1 rep max
  - » Leg press, 4 sets
  - » Leg extensions, 2 sets
  - » Leg curl, 2 sets (different from Monday)
  - » Core exercise, 2 sets
- **Wednesday:** all exercises with 1 minute rest between sets; using either time or reps; usually less than 50% of 1 rep max
  - » Low row, 2 sets
  - » Back exercises (different than those done earlier in the week), 2 sets each
  - » Triceps exercise (different than previous Thursday), 2 sets to failure
  - » Reverse hyper
- **Thursday:** upper body, 35-45% of max in weight with either bands or chains, to total no more than 75-80% of max at top of movement, 2-3 reps per set; 6-8 sets; rest between sets varying between 30 and 60 seconds.
  - » Biceps, 1-4 rep max, 2 sets
  - » Triceps, 1-4 rep max, 2 sets
- **Friday:** lower body, 35-45% of max in weight with either bands or chains, to total no more than 75-80% of max at top of movement, 2-3 reps per set; 6-8 sets; rest between sets varying between 30 and 60 seconds.

I used this training method from 1996 to 1999, the years when I was very actively competing. Today I would use a similar but different training regime. I like the method of Louie Simmons at Westside Barbell – a four-day-a-week program with a lot more rest compared to what I was doing in 1996. If I was competing today, I would follow that program. I would also follow it if I had more time in my schedule for training.

Between 1999 and 2003, I returned to my older training style because of its simplicity and the time factor. I retained my competitive strength until 2003 when I became a commercial property and second gym owner. I needed a lot of time to build the gym (planning, getting permits, construction, picking and purchasing equipment). My personal fitness training really suffered from missed workouts and lack of sleep. After the gym opened in 2004, I was able to more consistently train though with two gym locations, my time was still limited. I never was able to regain the level of strength and fitness I had prior to 2003, so I now focus on staying healthy and in good shape.

Avoiding Injury

Today I do not push my training as I once did. Whereas my attitude used to be all-or-nothing, now I train smart and stay within my comfort limits. If the training doesn't feel right that day, I back off or even stop so I won't injury myself. On other days, I know I can push harder, so I do.

When you sustain an injury, it affects your workouts and your fitness results. You either won't be able to train the injured muscle group at all, or only at a greatly reduced level and you'll lose the gains you made while overtraining.

Secret #24: Do your best to avoid injury.

My goal now is to be consistent, even if it means not training to my full potential. This has been hard for me because a big part of my past success is based on my desire to continuously improve and my love of a challenge. I can do 60 lbs., I want to do 70 lbs., then 80 lbs., and so on.) But training too aggressively puts me at risk for injury, which then compromises my ability to stay healthy and active.

CHAPTER 8

Injury Prevention and Rehabilitation

From my own personal experience and those of my clients, I have learned that injury prevention is critical and that it is based on each individual having the right exercise program. Beginning with an evaluation of risk versus reward and including many other components, a well-balanced exercise program is your best insurance against injury.

A well-balanced program means you are working opposing muscle groups evenly. Injury can be caused by many things: trauma, an accident such as a fall or even obesity. But in my experience, many problems in the skeletal system are the result of a muscular imbalance in opposing, supporting or surrounding muscles.

Here are examples of easy shoulder rehabilitation exercises that can be done at home. (The instructions for these exercises appear in the appendix). Doing these exercises routinely will rehab your shoulder to a point

Shoulder rehab exercise (especially
good for rotator cuff muscles)

Shoulder rehab exercise (especially good
for strengthening rear delt area.

where daily activities can be done without pain. I recommend the exercises be continued 2-3 times a week (3 sets of 20 reps each) indefinitely as a maintenance program. If pain recurs, it is probably because you stopped doing the exercises or suffered a major re-injury.

Secret #26: Most muscular discomfort and pain is the result of muscle imbalance.

A variety of problems can lead to muscular imbalance. An improperly-designed training program is one; so is failing to use proper form during training. An injury can lead to muscular imbalance, and muscular imbalance can cause injury.

When a muscle is injured, the brain takes it out of service to protect it and give it time to heal. This means that other muscles have to take over doing the work of the injured muscle, forcing them to work outside their normal capacity. The extra stress causes discomfort and may lead to additional injury.

What happens after an injured muscle heals? Rather than returning to work, it has to be retrained to work properly with other muscles in order to re-establish muscular balance. I have a theory to explain why this is so. After injury, a muscle gets weaker and some atrophy occurs. At the same time, the other muscles are getting stronger even as they are overstressed. Once the injured muscle recovers, it is much smaller and weaker than the other muscles and less able to do its work. With reconditioning, it gains strength and eventually is able to fully function.

When rehabilitating a muscle after injury, I always begin with little or no weight to allow the injured muscle to participate. I gradually increase the weight but never allow it to become too heavy for the rehabbing muscle. Too much weight too soon means that the stronger muscles will do all the work, leaving the rehabbing muscle in its weakened and atrophied condition.

Training for Muscular Balance

Recently I read an article listing the ten worst exercises for risk of injury. The bench press was on the list for causing shoulder injuries. I disagree with the article. It is improper training and muscular imbalance that causes injury, not the bench press exercise.

Guys love the bench press. Ask someone how much they can lift, and they'll tell you what they can bench press. In the gym, Monday is the unofficial bench press day because the chest is such an important muscle group for most guys. After a weekend out of the gym, starting the week off right means working the chest which means doing the bench press. If something keeps you from the gym for the rest of the week, at least you got in the bench press.

But what about the other muscle groups – aren't they just as important? Of course they are, even though many guys don't seem to think so. A few may be interested in arms or back, but what about rear delts? Wait a minute, they say. Rear delts? What's a rear delt? If I can't see it, it can't be that important. Besides, I'm probably working them while I'm doing something else.

Deltoid fly exercise showing proper position of elbows to work the rear delts.

Well, you're not. And by working your chest muscles and ignoring the upper back, you create a huge muscular imbalance.

I want to stay with the bench press for a while to illustrate my point. The primary muscle group involved when you bench press is the chest, and the secondary groups are triceps and shoulder. The shoulder muscle areas that need to be trained evenly are front, side and back deltoids. The bench press works the front and, to some extent, the side deltoids. But not the rear delts. The incline bench press works the front delts even more.

Let's say you are lifting 200 lbs. on the bench press. To do this, you use your chest and front deltoid muscles and triceps to bring the weight down to your chest and push it back up. Even if your chest muscles can't lift the weight from your chest, your front delts and triceps have still felt the stress.

Most people don't know what the rear delts are, and those who do know, don't know where they are or how to train them correctly. This is because the upper back muscles are much stronger than the rear delts, causing you to instinctively involve them by changing the angle of your elbows to be closer to your hips. Your instincts say *why are you working so hard; if you lower your elbows, the bigger muscles can help and make it easier.* Or for other exercises, you might use momentum or other muscle groups not intended to make the task easier.

We are no longer hunting and gathering for survival like our ancestors. Now we strengthen our muscles in more sophisticated ways with sophisticated equipment. We use good form and full range of motion, which requires more mental discipline while promoting much greater and safer holistic benefits.

Back to the rear delts. If you don't use good form or full range of motion, you'll find the exercise for the rear delts is easier because you've inadvertently engaged the upper back. To avoid this, you need to maintain good form by keeping the elbows above shoulder level and below the ears as the range of motion. Training the rear delts is the one exception to my rule of full range of motion. In this exercise only, do not allow the arms to go to full extension of the arms. Instead, stop at the point of full extension of the rear deltoids. The reason for this is that the rear deltoids have a short range of motion. If you go to full extension of the arms, you allow the rear delts to rest between each rep.

Secret #27: Don't use instinct to train. Train with your brain.

Learn to override your instincts not to make the workout easier, but to be safer, more efficient and effective. Learn the proper range of motion and stabilization and use only the intended muscles in the intended motion and at the proper speed. Do not use the amount of weight you are lifting as the sole measure of success. If you are using bad form, the weight you are lifting is irrelevant. The true test of strength is the amount of weight you can lift with proper form. Good form allows you to maximize the safety, efficiency and effectiveness of the exercise to realize all the benefits of resistance weight training.

Successful Olympic weightlifting is a combination of proper form (meaning you are engaging muscles for maximum benefit) and technique (such as timing, coordination and footwork). The lifts of Olympic weightlifting (the snatch and the clean and jerk) are less a test of pure strength than a test of strength combined with technique. In this sport, great technique + good strength will beat great strength + good technique. In contrast, competitive power lifting (bench press, squat, and deadlift) is a true test of strength. In this sport, great strength + good technique will beat great technique + good strength.

What all this means is that if you cheat by using bad form, you are hurting yourself. Using bad form (that is, engaging muscles other than those being trained) might mean that you can temporarily lift more weight on some exercises. But in the long term, you will actually be getting weaker overall. And if you're a competitive powerlifter, that means you'll be restricting your potential on the bench press, squat and deadlift, making you less competitive.

Traditional weightlifting exercises are designed around powerlifting and so respond better to proper form. But you can easily be fooled into thinking *more is better*, because bad form allows you to move more weight even though you are receiving less benefit. (There is one caveat – sometimes you need to relax proper form a little bit to continue to make improvements, but you must return to proper form and maintain it until your next sticking point.)

Let's return to the bench press to illustrate the full effect of muscle imbalance. The same guy who is not working his rear deltoids and therefore has created a muscle imbalance now starts doing front deltoid exercises on shoulder day. He fails to realize how much more developed the front delts are compared to the rear delts. And since the front delts are easier to train, he makes the muscle imbalance even worse.

Secret #28: Pay attention to muscle balance. Do not train a muscle just because you think you should or everyone else is.

The upper back is another area worth mentioning for muscle imbalance. Remember I said that using improper form to train rear delts will result in training the upper back muscles instead. If you inadvertently, through bad form, are working the upper back with weights meant for rear delts, you will be training the wrong muscle group (upper back instead of rear delts). The problem is that the upper back requires a much heavier weight than the rear deltoids because the upper back must be in balance with the chest muscles, not the front deltoids. By using the amount of weight intended for rear deltoids while training the upper back, the upper back will not be trained adequately to balance the muscles of the upper back and chest.

Here's an example: on back day, the exercises train the upper back (though many people neglect that muscle group). By letting the elbows drop too low below the chest line into the low row position, you are working an entirely different – and much stronger – primary muscle. Your instinct will tell you to use a range of motion that makes the exercise easier, but this makes the problem worse. You're now relying on the latissimus dorsi muscles instead of the upper back to handle the weight, and therefore not working the upper back muscles. This creates a muscle imbalance that can lead to shoulder pain, upper back pain, neck pain and possible injury.

One note to remember as you are reading: when I discuss a muscle being worked and mention only one muscle or muscle group, I'm doing that for simplicity. In every exercise, there is a primary or dominant muscle or group (the one I mention) and an additional, secondary set of muscles.

I hope you're starting to see how complex it is to train properly. Every

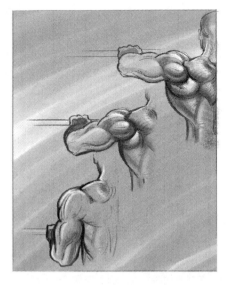

Top figure shows the position for the deltoid row or deltoid fly (working the rear delts) The middle figure shows the position for the high row (working the rhomboid muscles). The bottom figure shows the position for the low row (working the lats).

little detail makes a huge difference! Instead of building muscle, you end up with shoulder pain and bad posture. Now multiple the bench press and rear delt examples by every muscle group in the body and you'll see why it takes immense attention to detail to get it all right. My system is simple to understand but complex in the requirement to pay attention to details. And it's the attention to details that produces the results.

To help you learn and master the details for training each muscle group correctly, I encourage you to visit www.FitnessResults.com. What you'll find there are short videos, photos and written descriptions to help you perform exercises correctly for each muscle group. As a bonus, you'll also find exercises for rehabilitating muscles after injury.

Knees

Knees are a common problem area for many people. Some knee pain comes from other areas, such as unstable hips or ankles. Traditional leg exercises using the leg press strengthens the knees, hips and ankle. Often a proper leg workout will result in easing of aches and pains in the knees and balancing the muscles of the lower body.

Building a strong foundation is crucial to a successful resistance weight training program. If you were building a house, you would lay down a strong, well-engineered foundation to withstand the forces from the rest of the house. With a properly planned and executed foundation, there would be no limit to how big the house could be without crumbling.

Starting an exercise program is exactly the same. Begin with a properly-designed program and take the time necessary to build the foundation for long-term, sustainable success and limitless strength potential without compromising safety, effectiveness or efficiency. The key components of a solid foundation are learning proper exercise form and teaching your body the proper coordination and range of motion. Focus on form, not on the muscle being trained. If you have proper form, you will achieve better muscle development and strength safely. Begin with light weights so even the weakest muscles can begin to build strength, then move on to retraining all muscles to work properly together. Finish by developing muscle balance and harmony.

Building the foundation will go faster when you use the best exercises based on the available tools. If you are able to go to a gym for weight training, the leg press is the best tool for foundation-building – much better than a free squat with no apparatus, or a supported squat (holding onto something for balance), or a suspension squat (using body weight) or a machine squat. Let me explain why. Imagine a 45-year-old woman who leads a sedentary life who wants to lose weight, gain strength and feel better. She weighs 175 lbs., is 5"6" and has 32% body fat. Imagine if her trainer put her on the leg press and set the pin to 175 lbs. (her body weight). She would likely object because she'll be looking at the pin and realizing she's being asked to raise half the stack when much lighter weights are available. Common sense will tell her that she won't be successful at lifting half a stack, while she could be successful at less weight.

Starting with any kind of squat instead of the leg press is asking the woman to raise that 175 lb. half stack. By putting her in the leg press with a more reasonable 40 lbs. as a starting point, the trainer can assess her ability and plan the training regimen. Additionally, and just as important, the woman will start her training with success.

But suppose you don't have access to a leg press. You can still train your legs by using a substitute exercise such as an assisted squat (which I call a *sissy squat).* Rather than free form, a sissy squat lets you hold on to something (like the sides of a door frame) for balance and assistance in rising from the squat. To make it the best option available, you need to assess the risk of overtraining or injury and make adaptations. For instance, initially you can reduce the range of motion, increasing it gradually as you become stronger.

Secret #29: Women are far more likely than men to suffer a knee injury while engaging in the same sport. In fact, women athletes are over four times as likely to suffer an anterior cruciate ligament (ACL) injury than a male athlete.

Genetically, women have a muscle imbalance: their quadriceps are stronger than their hamstrings. When the quadriceps are engaged, the hamstrings are not automatically engaged. Because of the strong quadriceps and the failure to automatically engage the hamstrings, women are at risk for hyperextension which can cause injury.

Men naturally have better muscle balance between the strength of the quadriceps and hamstrings. When the quadriceps are engaged, the hamstrings are simultaneously activated, reducing the risk of hyperextension and injury.

Preventing knee injury is another reason to consistently exercise with a proper resistance weight training program, especially for women and young girls who participate in sports. Golfers and tennis players, who are prone to injuries of the shoulder, back, elbow, knee and ankle, can greatly reduce the risk of injury as well as improve their game by exercising with a proper resistance weight training program.

Core Muscles, Back Pain and Injury

In my opinion, the beginning of back pain and injury can often be traced to the exercises from physical education class or participation in sports, as well as the negative effects of sitting in class for hours every day. Consider bending over to touch your toes, a form of stretch. A safe passive stretch is always done with support, which is not the case with touching your toes. Similarly, sit-ups, which strengthen abdominal muscles and hip flexors, create muscular imbalance with the rest of the core muscles (lower back, obliques). This could be the beginning of a lifetime of an imbalanced core.

Core strengthening exercises have become very popular because people believe they will reduce the midsection, or help with back pain and injury. This belief comes in part from the hundreds of core-strengthening devices for sale, and the gyms where personal trainers instruct their clients to perform ab-specific exercises. But think about it for a minute: if the devices worked the way the good-looking people in the ads claim, or if the ab-specific exercises were truly effective, we would all have great abs.

The truth is that adding exercises specific to one or two core muscle groups creates an imbalanced core. The exercises not only don't help with the intended goal of displaying great abs, they increase the risk of chronic back problems, waste time and energy, and in the end, create a thicker midsection – the opposite of the desired result.

My clients achieve a stronger, balanced core passively by using proper form that requires core stabilization. Combine this with rising to the challenge of achieving new maxes, proper diet and rest, and my clients reduce their midsection and alleviate back pain.

So why do improper and potentially unsafe fitness exercises remain so popular? I think this is the reason. Imagine a high school football player who loves his sport and decides on a career as a coach. He attends college to earn a degree in exercise physiology and a teaching credential, and lands his first job as a high school football coach.

Of course he doesn't start as the head coach, but as an assistant. In that role, he has to learn the ways of the head coach which are familiar to him from his high school playing days. Even though these ways may contradict some of what he learned in college, the school team is doing fine, the coaching system seems to work, and the entire coaching staff is on board with the program. By the time our assistant coach becomes head coach, the current coaching system has been institutionalized and he no longer remembers so clearly what he learned in college. So the old ways never change and coaching systems don't evolve. I train a lot of high school football players and when I ask them about their training regimen, I find they are doing the same things I did when I played high school football over 30 years ago.

CHAPTER 9

Other Sources of Information for Your Fitness Results

I am very critical of fitness professionals, especially those with popular television shows, which send the wrong message about how to train for fitness. I don't watch much television, but when clients kept asking me for my reaction to what they had seen on TV, I had to take a look. I could not stand to watch more than a few minutes because what I saw constituted gross negligence in my mind. If I trained clients like the TV fitness gurus, I would be open to lawsuits. And I'd be guilty. I am certain that any true fitness professional would have the same reaction I did.

One of those TV actor-trainers has a tagline of *America's Toughest Trainer* and is endorsing all kinds of products. I'm not sure where the tagline comes from, but I beg to differ with it. I'm certain that in the military there are drill instructors that are way tougher. Anyone can put together a series of exercises to cause stress and couple that with yelling and screaming. It may be good TV, but it certainly isn't a good, productive workout or a healthy training regimen.

I was similarly disappointed in one of the organizations that certify professional trainers. In fact, it was the one where I obtained my first certification. At that time, the organization rated different media sources for credibility on providing health and fitness information. Then they sold out for what's trendy and popular by endorsing a celebrity trainer and selling a fitness certification with the trainer's name on it. If they had rated themselves for credibility as they used to do, they certainly would have had a very low score. This is a reminder to be vigilant and assess sources of information for yourself before you act.

My style of training is quieter but really much tougher – to push my clients to get the most out of each rep and each set, using deep concentration to maintain good form, and not to give up until the point of exhaustion at that time is reached.

Secret #30: Not all health and fitness information is credible, factual or relevant to you.

We live in a great time when modern technology gives us easy access to almost anything, where we can obtain information anywhere, any time, and on any topic. But notice that I said *information*. Not *good information* or *reliable information* or *accurate information*. Just *information*. In this section I'll discuss information sources, how to determine whether they are credible, factual and relevant for you, and the downside of our fast-paced lifestyle and easy access to so much information.

Let me start by assuring you that I am not a conspiracy theorist or the kind of person who sees the worst in everything. Instead, I'm a realist who uses good, old-fashioned common sense.

Common Information Sources

Media source	Type of information
Television	News, informercials, talk shows, reality show, sitcom, commercials
Radio	News, informercials, talk shows, commercials, disc jockeys
Newspapers	Articles, op/ed, advertisements
Magazines	Articles, editorials, advertisements
Social media	Experts, hobbyists, peers, friends, family, co-workers, fellow gym members
Government, federal	Surgeon General, Food & Drug Administration (FDA)
Professionals	Doctors, hospitals, insurance companies, workplace literature, private schools and colleges
People (face-to-face)	Family, friends, co-workers, anyone/anywhere

I have probably missed a few, but you get the idea.

Corporate Media

Let's put television, radio, newspapers and magazines – especially health and fitness magazines – in one group and call it *corporate media*. I'm not saying good journalism is dead, but you definitely have to pay attention to determine if it is credible, factual and relevant for you.

Corporate media has as its primary goal making money, not looking out for the best interest of its audience or educating the public. Corporate media puts out information people are interested in and takes in money by selling advertisements. It would not be in their best interest to air or publish a news segment or article that reflects negatively on one of their advertisers. Remember the idiom *don't bite the hand that feeds you.*

As I mentioned, I'm not a conspiracy theorist. Not everything aired or published by corporate media is bad or inaccurate. Sometimes the information is credible, factual and relevant for you. The challenge is to not accept things at face value, but dig deeper. Does the information come from a recognized professional in the field of the topic in question? Or is it from an expert in a different field? If the topic is nutrition but the doctor presenting the information is a doctor of kinesiology, you should take a closer look before assuming it is credible.

Some information comes from a credible source but isn't relevant to you. Here is a hypothetical example: a recognized expert in the field of weight loss cites a study in which a test group took a weight loss pill and had tremendous results, leading to the conclusion that the pill may be the answer to losing weight. The test group took one pill once a day for ten days and lost an average of 15 lbs. over that time period without exercise or cardio. All the information presented is factually accurate and presented by a credible source.

But here's where you need to dig deeper: the test group actually consisted of three body builders in the off season who were in bad shape. They had not competed in a while, had not been watching their diet, had been eating lots of sugary foods, and were 40 lbs. heavier than normal. Because they are body builders, they have lots of muscle and a high metabolic rate. By just eliminating sugar and watching their diet as they would to prepare for competition, they could easily lose 15 lbs. in 10 days (though most of it would be water weight). The corporate media has not lied to you; they just omitted some important facts and relevant information, making the reported results misleading.

To dig deeper into this story, you would need to find out more about who conducted the study (their background, training and affiliations), their motivation, how many total people participated in the study and their background, how long the study lasted and similar information. Then use your common sense to decide whether the conclusions are relevant to you and your situation.

My personal bias is to use information from corporate media as entertainment. If there is something that piques your interest, find out more information then apply common sense. A lot of health- and fitness-related information is faddish. Topics are hot for a while because people are curious and looking for a "magic bullet". Before it is determined whether the topic is safe or has any long-lasting value, everyone moves on to the next hot topic.

Government

A lot of information is published at all levels of government. Many people trust the Food and Drug Administration and similar governmental agencies to provide reliable information on nutrition, such as the well-known food pyramid. Unfortunately, the pyramid was not based on good science. Instead, it was influenced by agribusiness industry special interests and has recently been replaced by the current plate-and-cup illustration (which I have used in this book). The differences between the food pyramid and the plate-and-cup are dramatic, with the plate-and-cup being much closer to the nutrition program that I use for my clients. Be aware, though, that even with this improvement, some recommendations by the scientific team were not included in the revised nutritional guidelines.

I believe that people need to be responsible for their nutrition decisions. I don't like blaming fast food corporate giants like McDonald's for the obesity epidemic in this country, especially when the food pyramid emphasizes eating too many carbohydrates and not enough fat. People can decide for themselves whether it is a good idea to "super-size" If we are taught nutrition, health and fitness as topics in school, we will be better educated and able to make good choices. The trend to eliminate physical education from schools is definitely not the way to promote a healthy life style. I sometimes eat at McDonald's, but always look for something on the menu that fits within a nutritionally-balanced diet.

Although I am critical of the nutrition information and nutritional policies of the federal government, I do rely on their population studies. These studies take the population as a whole, subdivides it into demographic groups, then look at what happens to these groups over time. You can find out information such as the percentage of obesity for a certain age group and compare today's number to years past, tracking the changes for better or worse. And that's just one example; there is lots of other health and fitness information available. Not everything may be completely applicable to your situation but it can be a good resource for fact-checking and trends.

Professional Organizations

I have found that information from professional health and fitness industry organizations is very reliable. The information is written for their
members, not the general public. The information is intended to help
health and fitness industry professionals provide better services to their
clients. I frequently turn to organizations like the American College
of Sports Medicine (ACSM), the Aerobics and Fitness Association of
America (AFAA) and the International Health, Racquet and Sports Club
Association for information. I believe that all true industry professionals
should belong to one or more of these organizations so they have access to
this quality information.

Colleges and Universities

Some colleges and universities publish newsletters containing high
quality scientific information. Harvard Health, Stanford Medicine News,
Tufts University Health & Nutrition Letter are all excellent sources
of information.

Doctors

Doctors can be a great source of health information but not necessarily
for fitness. Here's an example: one of our personal training clients suffered
from knee pain that kept her from sleeping well because her knee ached
at night. Within a few weeks of starting resistance weight training, she no
longer had pain at night, was sleeping better, and didn't have to nap during
the day. On her next doctor visit, her doctor mentioned her weight loss
and asked how she had done it. When she told her doctor she was working
out with a personal trainer, the doctor congratulated her but suggested
she discontinue leg work because of her knee problem.

At her next workout, she announced that she was no longer going to
do leg workouts because her doctor had suggested it. I disagree but said
we would honor her doctor's suggestion. Within a few weeks her knee

pain had returned and she was again not sleeping well at night. She asked me whether she should go back to the leg workouts that had previously provided her relief. I asked her to first obtain her doctor's release and explained what would be done during the leg workouts. Her doctor gave her the release and within a short period, her pain was again relieved.

Your doctor can provide you with all kinds of educational material on many topics – weight loss, high blood pressure, diabetes, kidney stones, etc. But he might not be the right source of information on the benefits of resistance weight training.

Social Media

Social media is a double-edged sword. It is excellent for motivation and support from peers who share things like tips, ideas on meal preparation and recipes. But please don't rely on social media for professional advice. Young people who look great but lack professional experience dispense health and fitness advice to thousands of followers who take it as gospel truth even though it may be unsafe and not beneficial. Similarly, someone who has recently embraced a healthy lifestyle and lost a lot of weight wants to share their success with others but lacks the professional experience to provide sound advice. And this is not limited to those talking about health and fitness. People who compete in physique contests, bodybuilding, powerlifting or are celebrities anoint themselves experts and begin giving advice.

Don't fall for the hype. My niece Katie, who is newly engaged and recently graduated from college, wanted to go shopping for a wedding dress with her mom Judy, some friends and my wife Susie. Katie and her friends, who live out of town, stayed for a few days at our house and accompanied Susie on her morning walk with our dogs.

During the walk, Katie's college roommate, whose degree is in athletic training, shared with Susie the phone app they were using for personal training exercises. Susie was skeptical of the exercises, so asked me to evaluate them.

I am sad to say that the exercises were neither safe, effective, nor efficient. And I was shocked when Katie's roommate told me she was using the app because she did not know what she should be doing for exercise. This is a newly-minted college graduate with a degree in athletic training, who cannot formulate a training program, or at the very least tell the difference between a safe program and an unsafe program.

Secret #31: Having a college degree doesn't guarantee that the information will be applied.

I was also puzzled as to why the girls didn't turn to me for advice. I own a gym and have student interns. For all four years of college, I helped Katie and her roommate move in and out of college dorm rooms, carrying couches and tables and boxes up and down stairs. I took them out for breakfasts, lunches and dinners, yet neither girl sought my advice on personal training.

Instead, they turned to someone with an app who likely has limited experience and follow that person even though they should know better. That's the power of social proof or informational social influence – where people follow the action of others assuming that if everyone else is doing it, it must be right. The girls didn't use common sense nor wonder why, when as a society we are paying record amounts for health and fitness advice, we are in the worst overall state of health and fitness ever.

Don't listen to these self-proclaimed experts. I learned a lot while I was competing as a powerlifter. But I did not begin advising clients on health and fitness until I had 14 years of experience working out in the gym and had become a certified personal trainer.

Oh, yes, in case you're wondering: Katie found her wedding dress at the second place they visited.

Family and Friends

Use family, friends and co-workers as a referral source to find a personal trainer or gym or health and fitness professional. But before you settle on one, check to be sure the trainer is certified. A true professional trainer will always have a current certification because he or she is motivated by the desire to have the most relevant and current information in the industry. If the recommended trainer isn't certificated, keep searching until you find one who is.

My AFAA wallet certificate denoting my certification. I carry it with me at all times.

The Aerobics and Fitness Association of America (AFAA) provides its certified trainers with a wall certificate and a wallet card. To keep certification current, you have to complete continuing education units (CEU) which I always do. This is needed because since I first obtained my certification, there have been continuous changes and advancements in health and fitness.

In addition to the basic certification, I maintain numerous specialty certifications. One example is a multiple sclerosis (MS) certification (for which I get a listing in the directory of the National Multiple Sclerosis Society as being certified to train clients with MS). I am also certified for TRX suspension and Rip training; nutrition; special populations (children and seniors, pre- and post-natal).

Although I carry my AFAA certification card with me in my wallet, only once in the 20+ years since I became certified has anyone asked to see my certification. It is easy to assume that a trainer is certified, but I recommend that you always ask for proof of current certification. Also check to be sure that the certificate is good for no more than two years, and that it requires CEU credits. If this is not the case, the certification is not up to industry standards and is not credible.

Technology

Technology has made it easy and convenient to do so many things: communicate with family and friends, shop, or conduct research from the comfort of your home or office. But all this convenience has a price

– primarily the stress of being available 24/7. Cell phones beep, chirp and ring reminding you of a waiting text or e-mail. Friends and colleagues expect to be able to reach you any time of day. Social media updates come in and tease you to read them. Strangely, all this information may actually make it harder to find what you want or need.

Stress from technology overload affects our eating habits, our sleep and has a negative impact on the health and fitness of our entire society. Obesity is now an epidemic which in turn is causing a rise in diabetes. Instead of physical movement in the form of running or playing or exercise, children entertain themselves with cell phones, tablets and computers.

Because you are reading this book, I know you have taken responsibility for your own health and fitness. Please take the information in this book to heart and stay on the path to achieving your fitness results.

CHAPTER 10

Flexibility and Stretching

I know what you are thinking: stretching is easy; it's just boring. All I need to do is find a little more time to do my stretches. Or maybe you did find the time and you are stretching like crazy because most people think that if you can bend over and put your palms flat on the ground, that's being flexible. Or maybe you're doing yoga in lieu of resistance weight training because of misinformation.

Flexibility is important for injury prevention, improving balance, reducing pain and for sports performance. But did you know that your stretching program needs to be thought out with the same kind of mapping and predetermined destination as resistance weight training? A stretching program shouldn't be a compulsive, last minute effort because you heard some celebrity is doing it or you read an article in a magazine. Managing your flexibility requires the same considerations as a resistance weight training program: the stretches, a nutrition plan, and cardiovascular conditioning.

The question everyone has is how much flexibility is optimum. The answer is different for each individual, based on fitness level and goals and the types of activity you intend to engage in. Although there are many types of flexibility, I will limit my discussion to the three main types. If you want to explore others on your own, do so with a certified professional personal trainer, athletic trainer, physical therapist, or someone else with professional training in stretching techniques. This is the only way to achieve a specific goal safely.

Three Main Types of Flexibility

These are the three main types of flexibility:

1. *Dynamic functional flexibility:* moving a body part through a full range of motion using only the muscles required for that body part. Desirable for sports that require long, explosive movements such as throwing, running, jumping, high kicking.
2. *Static functional flexibility:* holding an outstretched position without support. Ideal for dancers and gymnasts as it requires muscle strength to maintain flexibility.
3. *Static inactive flexibility:* holding an outstretched position with support. Good for power sports like weightlifting and wrestling if done with the right technique.

How flexible should you be? To answer that question, you must know what you want to achieve. Some possibilities are good health and fitness; injury prevention; rehabilitation after injury; alleviation of pain; increased balance; or a combination of several factors. The optimum amount of flexibility to aim for depends on your goals.

Interestingly, the more flexibility you have in a joint, the less stable it is. Conversely, the less flexibility, the greater the joint stability. All joints do not require the same degree of flexibility. In fact, each joint can have a different flexibility level depending on the goal.

Secret #32: Flexible joints are less stable, and stable joints are less flexible.

So the answer to the question *How flexible do I need to be* is: just a little more flexible than the demand of range you require for a given activity – in other words, just a slight surplus of flexibility.

For most people past the age of 50 (which includes Baby Boomers), the goal is to be healthy and active with minimal aches and pains. This group has no desire to participate in highly competitive sports or other activities, but still loves to hike, walk, ride bikes, kayak, travel or engage in other moderate activities. I myself fit into this group. For these people, the goal is average flexibility of all three types – dynamic functional, static functional and static inactive. Expressed on a scale of 1 to 10 with one being no flexibility and ten being a contortionist, five would be the flexibility goal. This provides good joint stability and protection while simultaneously allowing for adequate movement with no restrictions on activity plus the benefit of injury prevention, increased balance and pain reduction.

For those whose goal is to enhance sports performance or engage in a demanding activity, you must always remember to balance the risk to the reward. As the goal to achieve greater flexibility goes up, so does the potential for injury. A well-thought-out plan based on sound knowledge and corrected executed greatly reduces the risk of injury.

Any flexibility plan should be designed around a resistance weight training program because as flexibility increases, muscles must be stronger and better conditioned to provide joint stability. As your strength increases, you'll need to build in an amount of flexibility surplus so you are never performing at the limits of your range of flexibility. Being at the limit of flexibility puts you at risk for a stress injury and prevents you from realizing peak performance at the limits of range. Having as little as a 5% surplus of flexibility will increase overall performance while reducing the risk of injury. Maximizing sports performance and safety requires looking at each joint separately to determine the type and amount each requires.

Flexibility training is similar to resistance weight training in that everyone's goals are different. One athlete might focus on explosive power, while another focuses on endurance. Like strength training, even though each sport requires a different type and range of flexibility, the fundamentals are the same. You need a balance of the three types of flexibility.

Factors of Flexibility

In life, there are things we can control and things we can't, including individual flexibility. Genetic factors have a major impact on your flexibility, meaning you may never be able to do the splits no matter how much you stretch and how hard you try. Or you may be prone to joint injury because you have too great a range of motion and not enough joint stability to protect it. While some genetic factors can be controlled and others can be enhanced, your flexibility goals should take your natural tendencies into account.

The genetic factors affecting flexibility are:

- *Bone structure.* Some people – think of contortionists – have hypermobility, or joints that can move beyond the normal range of motion. Some people called this being *double jointed.* In fact, there aren't two joints, just unusually-shaped bone endings. Besides hypermobility, unusual bone endings can also cause a decrease in normal range of motion (hypomobility). Hypermobility can affect one or more joints.
- *Connective tissue.* Elasticity, length and attachments points of the tendons, ligaments and muscles affect flexibility. Range of motion can be restricted by excessive muscle mass, body weight or fat which get in the way of proper movement.

Stretching

Now that you understand the types of flexibility and what affects them, you are in a better position to determine your specific flexibility goals which you will achieve with the right type of stretching using the proper technique, good form and correct duration. (And you thought stretching would be easy – LOL.) What follows is a discussion of six types of stretching and the benefits of each.

Ballistic stretching (**or** *warming up*) is a form of passive or dynamic stretching that uses a bouncing motion to move in or out of the stretch. It is not considered either effective or safe, and I do not recommend it as it can cause injury with no reward. Many people who use ballistic stretching don't even know they are doing so, like the person who bends over to touch their toes and bounces to create rebound energy to increase range of motion.

Dynamic stretching is a controlled movement of speed and range, stopping gently at the limits of range of motion. An example is getting out of bed in the morning with a sore lower back. You stand up and do a slow twist side-to-side, gradually increasing range of motion but being careful not to push or exceed the range limit. After a few minutes your back feels loosened up and better. Athletes often use dynamic stretching before playing their sport or engaging in strenuous activity, using slow range of motion activities similar to the ones they will be using in the sport or activity. There are also calisthenics that incorporate dynamic stretching. In weight training, I use the same exercise we will be performing as part of the warmup process for each muscle group. This consists of a very light weight for 8-12 reps at a controlled speed and movement. This is dynamic stretching for that range of motion, in preparation for max sets.

Active stretching is what I call *static functional stretching:* holding a stretch position for 5-15 seconds without support or assistance other than the agonist (*i.e.,* contracting) muscle required to support the position. This allows the antagonist (*i.e.,* the opposing) muscle to relax and elongate which makes it stronger. Active stretching is common in yoga.

Passive stretching is what I call *static inactive stretching:* moving slowly to a comfortable supported stretched position, holding it for 20 seconds, then resting and repeating 3-4 times. This is a very common stretching technique because it is what we were taught in school. It is a good stretch to relieve muscle spasms and cramps, but not very effective for increasing range of motion. Passive stretching should only be done after a workout.

Isometric stretching involves the resistance of muscles by tensing the supported stretched muscle. It is only recommended for athletes or others who want or need to develop strength. The added stress of the contraction increases the risk of injury. Athletes competing in bench press that requires a pause at the bottom of the movement followed by maximal force to raise the bar without being able to use the rebound effect of a bounce of the bottom use isometric stretching. An isometric stretch begins like a passive stretch, but once in the stretched position, you contract the muscle, hold for 7-10 seconds, then relax for 20 seconds. This stretch allows for a greater amount of muscle fibers to be lengthened and to maintain the lengthening, providing greater muscle flexibility while promoting stability and tension in the joint. Isometric stretching should only be done after a workout.

PNF (proprioceptive neuromuscular facilitation) stretching is a technique combining passive and isometric stretching. It is a way to develop what I call *static functional stretching* and is a very effective technique when done with a certified professional. You should not do PNF stretching on your own, and only after a workout.

A Client Challenges Me on Stretching

My client Kevin was the head coach of his son's Little League baseball team. One day Kevin asked me for the best warmup exercise for his team before a practice or game (which includes dynamic stretching). I gave him my advice, and he followed up by asking about passive stretching exercises. I said the players should stretch passively *after* practice or a game, not before.

Kevin didn't agree, and said so. I responded that if he already knew the answer, why had he asked me the question. He said that my answer confused him. Kevin is an Anaheim Angels season ticketholder and regularly attends home games, arriving early to watch warmup. He observes that during warmup, the Angels players always do passive stretching. I said that by passively stretching pre-game, they are reducing their potential performance. Kevin still wasn't convinced. He mentioned that the Angels players make millions of dollars and have access to great trainers.

With a smile, I told Kevin that if the players trained with me, they would do even better. Then Kevin and I reviewed the point I'd made previously in this book in this section (Flexibility and Stretching), and he agreed that my method makes more common sense.

Kevin's confusion arises from a general misconception that passive stretching is the only type of stretching and the most effective for improving flexibility. Many people think *the more flexible, the better,* so I have to educate people, including Kevin, about stretching and flexibility.

Secret #33: Being good at a sport - even at the professional level - doesn't mean the athlete is using the best training methods.

My Recommendations and Thoughts on Stretching

Would you have guessed that flexibility would be so complex? You need all the information presented in this section in order to make good choices for your personal stretching program. Remember that when developing your program, you need to put as much care into defining your goals as you did with your weight training program.

(Most of my clients do not feel the need to have a flexibility program separate from their resistance weight training program. This is because I design into their programs flexibility maintenance and conditioning using dynamic stretching.)

You may be thinking that I've gone into too much detail in this section. I did so because most people don't realize that greater flexibility means less stable joints and therefore a greater risk of injury. On the other hand, safety and performance requires a flexibility surplus, but not one that is too big. A large flexibility surplus diminishes performance by wasting energy because muscles have to work harder to support the joints. A long distance runner with a large surplus of flexibility will not achieve optimal running efficiency because of wasting energy on joint support.

My recommendation for people whose goal is to be healthy and active with minimal aches and pains is to participate in a resistance weight training program using the recommendations and principles in this book. That will provide enough flexibility conditioning in your 3 x 30 minute weekly workouts to give you the benefits of injury prevention, improved balance, pain reduction and sports or activity performance. What I have found in over 100,000 personal training sessions is that most of my clients do not need additional stretching as a regular routine.

When I begin training a new client, I educate them on things I recommend that they do on their own – things they should be able to do safely and properly without supervision, like making good nutrition choices. I can provide education, support and motivation, but ultimately each client must make his or her own choices, whether it is nutrition or stretching. Though I could schedule an additional 20-minute appointment after each training session for stretching, there is not enough value or need for my clients to invest that time. By providing education, including demonstrating proper technique, my clients can safely stretch on their own unless they develop an issue that requires my assistance.

Some of my new clients who haven't done a resistance weight training program before start doing the wrong type of stretching in between sets. I must educate them not to do passive stretching before or during the workout, but to wait until the workout is complete. They often reply that they feel tight and need to stretch, to which I respond that tightness during weight training doesn't mean you lack flexibility. It might mean that you have fullness from added blood flow to the affected muscles or from delayed onset muscle soreness (DOMS). In addition, many clients have an awareness of their body and muscles that they never had before, and they aren't used to it. Over time they adapt to the feeling and even start to crave the feeling because they know it represents a healthy, active, more flexible body.

I'm not arguing for never adding an additional stretching program, or never doing stretching after a workout. Particularly if you have developed a muscle imbalance or spasm due to a poorly designed workout program or working out with bad form; inactivity; sitting for too long or in a bad position; sleeping on a bad mattress or in a bad position; or from injury, you should stretch for rehabilitation. But if everything is going well and you are feeling good, there is no need to create more stress by spending time doing an activity that provides no additional benefit in your life.

If your goal is to enhance performance in a sport or engage in a demanding activity, then it might be necessary to add a stretching session to your resistance weight training program, provided it is well thought out and takes into account all that I've presented in this section, including balancing the risk and reward.

If you are not participating in a resistance weight training program at all, or have a poorly designed or executed workout routine using short range of motion and bad form, you will develop unevenly conditioned and strengthened muscle groups. This will lead to muscle imbalance and increased risk of injury. You will also have a false sense of your true strength, meaning you might lift something so heavy you go past your conditioning point and risk injury to your unconditioned muscle groups and overstress your conditioned muscle groups. Working out with bad form causes overtraining which leads to small muscle tears, scar tissue buildup and risk of more severe injury. So you *could* try using a form of stretching regularly before and after each workout to counter the improper exercise program and bad form. Or, you could take the easier and better path by doing a weight training program with proper form in the first place.

It is never too late to take charge of your health and fitness or your flexibility. Just three 30-minute workouts a week using a properly-designed program of resistance weight training and executed with good form will give you most of what you need for a healthy, active life. It is hard to find good, credible information. If you haven't been correctly educated, you could be misled into doing things that will waste your time and perhaps cause a negative effect on your life. There is no substitute for using common sense to make good choices.

Foam Rolling

Foam rolling. It sounds like some kind of acrobatic activity, and when you first try it, you'll think that acrobatics should be a prerequisite.

I first heard of foam rolling at an IHRSA (International Health, Racquet and Sports Club Association) trade show in Los Angeles in 2012. This show is for health and fitness industry professionals, with experts in the field and sponsored athletes showcasing their products. I like to attend because it provides a good way for me to find out what's new in the industry.

IHRSA Show

Let me set the stage. I was walking down an aisle at the trade show when I noticed a booth for the Rumble Roller. This is a foam roller on steroids, though I didn't know it at the time. There was a lot of activity around the booth, which caught my interest. The booth was full of yoga enthusiasts who were using foam rolling as a form of self-massage. Lots of thin, limber people were watching a demonstration, so I joined them. The instructor, the inventor of the Rumble Roller, was demonstrating the technique, and I was intrigued by his description of myofascial release. (The fascia is the sheath of connective tissue enclosing a muscle. Myofascial release is a treatment that releases tension in the fascia.)

When the demonstration ended, the instructor asked me if I had ever tried rolling. I said I hadn't, so he encouraged me to try. I was reluctant because it didn't look like the sort of thing that a 5'10", 285-lb. power lifter should be doing for the first time in front of an audience. (Remember all those thin, limber people in the audience?) I thought I'd learn about it and try it in my gym with no one around.

But my wife was with me, and she wasn't going to walk away. She asked why I didn't try it right then because it looked like fun. To be a good sport,

I agreed to try. (Of course my wife walked to the back of the crowd, leaving me all by myself.) No one else wanted to join in, so the instructor took me through the whole embarrassing routine by myself, with everyone else watching. It wasn't as bad as I expected, and I survived with a shred of dignity. I even surprised a lot of people, including myself, on how well I was able to do the exercise, especially since it was my first time.

I would have preferred this as an introduction to foam rolling rather than what I went through.

This is a description of foam rolling: the equipment is a piece of dense, hard form, 6 inches in diameter and either 12 or 36 inches long.

You lay the roller on the floor or put it against the wall (for less pressure). Then you lay or lean on it, perpendicular to the roller, and roll your body over the roller in short sections. You stop at places of pain or

6" white foam roller, vibrating roller, Rumble roller

discomfort until the discomfort subsides, then move on to the next spot of discomfort, called a *trigger point*. The goal is to move through the range of motion with minimal discomfort. The more discomfort, the more you need to roll. It can take a while to master the coordination to roll effectively, moving from body part to body part across the entire body. The use of foam rolling is steadily evolving with new techniques that incorporate stretching with rolling.

The Rumble roller has knobs on the surface and comes in different densities. There are other brands as well, including a vibrating roller and small hand-held ones. Some people use a hand ball for smaller areas.

If your time permits, I recommend adding one rolling session a week to your workout, especially if you are having discomfort. Self-myofascial release is potentially a good idea for muscles that have been stressed after a workout to prevent myofascial pain syndrome.

CHAPTER 11

The Importance of Resistance Weight Training as We Age

Years ago, when my gym Fitness Results was a new business, I participated in community events as a way of marketing the gym. One of the events we did was the San Dimas Street Fair. We had a booth, and offered a prize of personal training to be raffled off at the end of the event. The only requirement to get in on the raffle was to fill out a card giving contact information.

When people walked by the booth, I asked them if they would like to complete the card for a chance at winning personal training sessions. Here's what I heard from older people:

- "I'm too old for personal training. That would be something my grandkids might be interested in".
- "That's not for me; I'm too old for that."

The Fitness Results street fair booth in the early 1990s. Monique, whose story I mentioned in an earlier section, is helping in the booth. I'm on the right in the green shirt (matching my green Fitness Results booth sign) and Max Muscle pants. At 5'10" and 290 lbs., I'm making a real fashion statement (LOL).

- "I don't need to exercise anymore."
- "I can't do that at my age."

I answered that they needed to exercise *more* than their grandchildren, that they were still young and healthy, and that as we age, it is even more important to stay physically active and participate in weight training. But my words fell on deaf ears because so many older people have a preconceived notion that after a certain age, you have to give in to the effects of aging.

Here are some ways that weight training counteracts the effects of aging:

- Increases bone density
- Prevents muscle loss
- Promotes better brain function and improved memory
- Promotes more youthful skin
- Increases balance and flexibility

- Improves energy levels
- Improves sleep
- Helps with disease control such as lowering cholesterol, preventing heart disease and diabetes
- Improves quality of life as well as life span

Secret #34: You are never too old to become more youthful and make a positive change in your health and fitness.

The health and fitness industry agrees with me on this topic. Because the Baby Boomer generation is so large and is now experiencing the effects of aging, the health and fitness industry is working hard to change the idea that we are helpless and destined to live out our days with gradually decreasing ability. Every day brings new information highlighting the benefits of exercise. So by living a healthy life style that includes resistance weight training, you can remain active, enjoying activities much longer than you may have thought possible.

Weight loss and body fat percentage

Maintaining a healthy weight and body fat percentage is important at any age, but especially as you get older. You can avoid or reduce the risk of developing diabetes, cardiovascular disease and cancer as well as keep your blood pressure and HDL/LDL cholesterol levels within normal limits.

Losing weight and gaining muscle is fairly easy for those under age 26. I have had several female clients in that age range that went from 28% body fat to 17% in less than four months. Rarely have I seen anyone past the age of 30 achieve similar results as fast. Instead, it takes eight months (double the amount of time) to achieve 17% body fat. Clients over the age of 40 take even longer and must put in more work and dedication. After the age of 50, it is possible to reduce body fat percentage to that level, but very rare. For 60 year olds, it becomes nearly impossible.

Secret #35: Never stop working on your health and fitness, but if you do, begin again ASAP!

The lesson from this is to maintain weight and body fat percentage in a healthy range throughout your life. But if you find you have gotten past what is considered healthy, don't give up or settle. Return to it as soon as you are able.

The example of 17% body fat is just that – an example. I'm not advocating that as a life goal. In fact, for most 50-year-old women, 22% body fat is a much more desirable and achievable goal. Also remember that body fat percentage is not the only measure of good health. Someone with a low body fat percentage who is not engaging in resistance weight training could be less healthy than someone with a higher body fat percentage who is doing resistance weight training.

I have several female clients who began training with me when they were in the early 60s and who had nearly 40% body fat (which put them in the very unhealthy "obese" range). Several years later, they had lowered their body fat to around 28% and leveled off. They look healthy and fit, have great energy, and can do things now that they could not do in their 40s.

There's a reason for this. As we age, we automatically lose muscle mass, which leads to a snowball effect. As muscle strength declines, we do less and become less active, resulting in still more muscle loss. The cycle repeats, speeding up muscle loss beyond that of natural aging. Before you know it, what used to be so easy you took it for granted becomes difficult or impossible to do. Something as basic as getting up off the ground requires additional points of contact (hands, knees) to complete the maneuver. Even rising from a chair becomes a problem, requiring a swinging motion of the upper body, hands pushing, and perhaps something to grab on to.

A major factor in longevity is maintaining leg strength. Loss of leg strength leads to a downward spiral: you become less mobile, then less coordinated, then suffer weakened core strength, followed by more loss of overall strength and coordination. Loss of muscle strength due to aging is called *age-related sarcopenia.* Between the ages of 27-40, people typically lose 10% of their muscle mass. From age 40-50, the loss of muscle mass increases to 15%. For ages 50-60, the loss is a whopping 30%, which continues in each subsequent decade. By the time you reach the age of 70, you could have lost more than 50% of your muscle mass.

And not only do you lose muscle mass, you also lose coordination and are more likely to develop osteoporosis, or thinning of the bones. Between the ages of 40-50, women can lose as much as 20% of their bone density, and an additional 10% for each additional decade. Osteoporosis is not confined to women, either. Men also lose bone density (though typically not at the same rate as women).

If you do not take preventive steps, the loss of muscle mass and bone density increases the likelihood that your 70s, 80s and 90s, you will not be able to do all the things you want to do with friends and family. It also subjects you to the risk of falling, which can have catastrophic consequences for the elderly. By participating in a proper resistance weight training program as outlined in this book and adopting a balanced diet containing adequate protein, you can maintain good coordination, drastically reduce muscle loss, and lessen the risk of developing osteoporosis.

You may be surprised at how easy it is to keep maintain your coordination and strength. Many senior residential facilities offer an exercise program using resistance bands. In as little as two weeks, participants drop down one assisted device, such as from a walker to a cane or a cane to not needing assistance. Since two weeks is not enough time to improve strength enough to account for this difference, the improvement is attributable to better coordination.

Because I began weight training as a teenager and was always conscientious about my health and fitness, I defied the aging process for a while. Here's a story that illustrates my point.

After my brother Daren graduated from the police academy and was hired as a police officer, he naturally wanted to celebrate. His friend Scotty, one of our workout partners, went with my brother to a restaurant, and later I joined them.

My brother Daren is on the left, workout partner Scotty in the middle, and me on the right. We were always celebrating something. This picture was taken after one of my competitions.

When I arrived, they were having a beer. I've never been much of a drinker, not because I don't approve, but because I'm dedicated to my health and fitness program. While training, I promised myself I would not drink alcohol the day before or the day after a training day. Because I was training seven days a week, I never drank alcohol and never developed a taste for it.

But here I was at a restaurant with my brother and training buddy for a celebration. When the waitress came to the table, I ordered a beer and she asked to see my ID. My brother and Scotty asked her what was up, since she hadn't carded them. She said that I looked too young to be drinking a beer! I happily showed her my ID, proving that I was 40 years old.

I mention this now because of my theory of good health. If you are in great health in during your early- to mid-20s and maintain that level without altering your fitness routine, you can maintain hormone and muscle levels closer to your body's peak levels. But as you age, and particularly if you have lapses in your training or stop training altogether, your body will catch up to the normal aging level.

Shortly after that celebration for my brother, I purchased the building that houses my gym. It was almost exactly a year from the day I closed escrow until my gym opened for business. During that time, my personal fitness suffered tremendously. For the first time since I began lifting weights, I did not train seven days a week. Most weeks during that year, I didn't work out at all. I also got less sleep than usual – some nights as little as 2-3 hours. Had I gone back to that same waitress after that year, she would have carded me. Although I did not lose all my youthful appearance, I did lose a lot.

A few years later, I fractured my back, then had to have three surgeries for hernia repair. Once again, I could not work out for long periods of time. I lost even more of my youthfulness and though the gap has not completely closed (I still look good for my age), it isn't as dramatic as it once was.

(By the way, I had all three hernia repairs at once – two abdominal and one inguinal on Friday morning. I was at work the next Monday at 5 am, not missing a single day of work. I figured that if I was going to be hurting after the surgery, I might as well have some company.)

Now for some good news. I believe that the opposite result can also happen. If you have not been taking care of your health and fitness and then begin a health and fitness program, you can regain some of your youthfulness. I have a couple (Nancy and Patrick) who are clients. They began working out with me in October 2009. Just recently Patrick told me a story about taking his 97-year-old father for a doctor's visit. The doctor's nurse assumed Patrick was the grandson, not the son. When told Patrick was 68 years old, she was amazed, as she assumed he was much younger. (I kidded Patrick that if it was 2009, before he started training with me, the nurse would have assumed he and his dad were brothers – LOL.)

Here's more proof based on Patrick and Nancy's experience. For years they have enjoyed a yearly vacation at Laguna Beach. Although they park their car and walk all week, they were not fit enough to manage the hilly streets of the city. After a year of training, they went on vacation and reported some exciting news: they could walk anywhere they wanted, and in fact were enjoying the challenge of ever-steeper hills. During the first 15 months of training, Patrick lost 90 lbs., gained muscle, and lowered his body fat percentage to an acceptable level.

Patrick and his wife Nancy in 2009
before they started training

Patrick: 6'0'

Comparison at ages 17, 62 and 63 years old

	1964 – 17 years old	2009 – 62 years old	2010 – 63 years old
Weight	206 lbs.	278 lbs. (+ 72 lbs.)	206 lbs. (-3 lbs.)
Chest	44.75"	51" (+ 8")	43" (-1.75")
Waist	35"	50.5" (+11.5")	39" (+4")
Thigh	26.5"	28.5" (+5.5")	23" (-3.5")
Biceps	13.75"	15.5" (+2")	13.5" (-0.25")

Who says there is no fountain of youth – after gaining 72 lbs. of weight throughout his adult life, at age 64, Patrick was back to his 17-year old youthful weight!

Young guy, old bike: Patrick at age 22 with his 1953 Harley Davidson Panhead in a 1947 frame. (1947 is the year he was born.)

Old guy, young bike: Patrick at age 64 with his brand new 2011 Harley Davidson Dyna Street Bob.

Another couple, Nick and Fosca, also had good results. They were in their late 70s and experiencing all kinds of health issues, including mobility problems. They provided a doctor's release for training and we got started. The first day of "weight training" (which was only range-of-motion exercises with no weights), I took them to the treadmill. I showed them how to walk on the machine and set it for the slowest pace – barely moving. After only three minutes, they had to stop. The next workout they lasted for ten minutes and went at a slightly faster pace. By the sixth workout day, they were managing a full 30 minutes at a normal pace. In less than two weeks, they had gone from barely being able to manage short distances to having almost no limitations. It didn't take much longer before they were doing things and feeling better than they had in decades.

Beginning a health and fitness journey based on the recommendations and philosophy in this book will lead you down a path away from common age-related risks of heart disease, Type 2 diabetes, stroke, some cancers, osteoporosis, dementia and depression. If you are a Baby Boomer, right now is the perfect time to take charge of your health and fitness. So many retired people talk about all the doctors they visit. It is as though they are still working instead of being retired, but going to doctors instead of to a job. With each doctor visit, they are working to keep their body functioning at a tolerable level. Instead, they could be spending as little as 30 minutes three days a week to improve their health and fitness and enjoy their retirement.

I'm a car guy – I love old classic cars, especially those that have had a full rotisserie restoration to like-new condition. Sometimes the restored cars look even better than the day they originally came off the assembly line. A classic restored car has survived over time and shows the unique and distinct characteristics of age. I like to think of my clients over the age of 55 as also undergoing a rotisserie restoration. I have clients who are stronger and more fit in their 60s than they were in their 20s. Gary began training with me at the age of 60. He was an avid golfer and set a goal of qualifying for the senior golf tour when he retired at age 65. He had not worked out since playing college football, so in the beginning he wasn't very strong, had poor endurance and was easily fatigued. He had kept measurements from high school athletics showing how much weight he lifted when he began playing college football. Because of training with me, before his 65th birthday, he hit his high school weight and established new maxes that were better than when he played college football. And yes, he achieved his dream of playing on the senior golf tour as a professional golfer.

Secret #36: You are never too old to improve your fitness and health.

CHAPTER 12

Cardio Training and Fitness Results

You may be wondering, "What is this guy talking about when he says you only have to weight train, eat well and get a good night's sleep. What about cardio?" This section will answer your questions.

Understand that I'm not suggesting you skip cardio. Instead, I want you to shift your focus to building your weight training foundation and stop wasting your valuable time worrying about fitting cardio into your busy schedule. Spend your time building a foundation, not creating unnecessary stress.

To reiterate: you control your weight through diet, not cardio! Use cardio to improve and maintain a healthy cardiovascular system. Yes, at times cardio can contribute to weight loss, provided you are doing it properly and have a good fitness foundation supporting it. But most of the time, I find that this is not the case, and the cardio program you are doing may actually be detrimental to your goals.

Wrong Reasons for Doing Cardio

- *Weight reduction.* Using cardio for weight reduction may hinder your weight loss goal if not done with the proper foundation program.
- *Build muscle.* Cardio is not effective for building muscle. Muscles are built by creating more stress than the muscle is used to, thereby stimulating the muscle to adapt to the new stress. During our waking hours, we walk and stand a lot which stimulates muscle strength and growth. Our muscles are already well adapted to this daily stress, and we are in maintenance mode. Given this, it would require a consistent, huge amount of time to realize only a modest improvement in muscle development

Cardio is one component of your overall health and fitness program but not the focus.

Positive Reasons for Doing Cardio

- *Cardio contributes to a health and fitness program.* However, the cardio must be the proper type and intensity in order to make the contribution to your health and fitness program.
- *Improve cardiovascular health.* This is a very good reason to do cardio, provided the cardio is the proper type, duration and intensity.
- *Improve cardio vascular condition.* This, too, is a very good reason, though again I caution you to make sure it is the proper type, duration and intensity or it won't contribute to your overall health and fitness program.
- *Sports performance.* As long as you understand the risk versus reward, go for it!

I love to ride my mountain bike, though I don't ride as much as I used to before I broke my back. I've always said *It's all about choices,* and on that day I made a series of bad choices – pretty common when you hear stories of injuries.

For Success in Cardio, Learn to Pace Yourself

You know that I don't claim to be the sharpest tool in the shed. On the day in question it was raining hard. I can be a little obsessive, and I needed to get my ride in. So I decided to ride my bike alone, even though my wife cautioned me not to – *Strike One*.

When I arrived at the entrance to the trail I wanted to ride, the gate was locked because of the rain. So I decided to access the trail at a place without a gate. That part of the trail wasn't maintained, but I'd used it before – *Strike Two*.

That section of the trail is very steep, twisty and slick, making it difficult in good conditions. The rain made the trail extremely slippery, and as I came around one of the very tight left-hand corners, there was a deep, wide crevice etched by the flow of rain water. I was unable to stop, so I tried to bunny-hop over the crevice. I came up short. My front tire hit the far side of the crevice, and the next thing I knew, I was doing a flip in the air. I landed on my back still clipped to my bike. I was stunned but seemed okay. I had a hard time unclipping from my bike because of the mud. I broke the seat off the carbon fiber seat post, and broke off the rear derailleur – *Strike Three*. With a broken back, I had to push my bike a couple of miles home. I was very lucky that this was the extent of what happened.

When I stopped competing and didn't work out as hard as I used to, I started riding my bike again. While competing, I did not do any additional cardio because I didn't want to lose muscle (which can happen with cardio) and there was no need as my regular training regimen allowed me to maintain great cardio condition. But when I stopped competing and my training was no longer as hard, I felt the need for more cardio conditioning.

Since I enjoy mountain bike riding, I decided to use that for my cardio. One of my buddies is a great rider, and since I'm not as good as him, it is a challenge to keep up – something I like. It is also a way for me to exercise without distraction, since when I'm exercising at the gym, people often ask me questions.

I'm a pretty good rider for a 5'10" guy who weighs 285 lbs. (Mountain bike riding is not a big guy sport). Once I went riding with one of my advertising sales reps, a 175-lb. guy who competed in triathlons. He'd never been mountain bike riding, so I loaned him one of my bikes (I have way too many of them) and off we went. After a short time, the guy is dying and wonders why he can't keep up with a big powerlifter. I told him that I know my limits and the trail. I know how to pace myself and stay below my lactic acid threshold to be consistent. I know the trail – when it goes uphill and when I can conserve energy going downhill; when I can push the pace and when not to. And I'm always in the right gear for the situation. But after a few rides, the triathlete will figure out what I know, and then I won't stand a chance of keeping up.

So remember me and the triathlete when you are starting a cardio routine that requires long distance and duration: pace yourself!

For a while I had a Life Fitness rowing machine in the gym. Everyone complained that it was too hard to use because they hadn't learned to pace themselves. They would row like crazy and burn out fast. You must slow down and pace yourself, especially when adding upper body to the cardio routine. That raises your heart rate quickly because the upper body muscles lack the blood delivery system of the lower body, which needs it for walking.

I understand that mountain bike riding may not be the perfect cardio solution for me. But I have considered all the tradeoffs, including loss of muscle – acceptable to me as I already am strong enough that getting stronger increases my risk of injury/

I also enjoy walking and hiking with my wife and dogs, and do much more of that since my accident. If I was still competing and found that I needed more cardio conditioning while maintaining maximum muscle, I would do HIT training (high intensity training) like running wind sprints.

All Cardio is Not Equal

- *High-intensity/short duration or HIT* training is great for maintaining muscle and cardiovascular conditioning. Just four minutes of proper HIT training has more cardiovascular benefit than one hour of moderate cardio. The drawback to HIT training that uses cardio equipment is that most equipment is not designed properly for correct HIT use. The treadmill takes too long to achieve up and down speed, so you need to switch to running outside on a track. The Tabata study used stationary bikes – 20 seconds of max effort, 10 seconds of rest for an 8-set cycle for a total of four minutes.

- *Low intensity/long duration* is good for the average person. Go for a walk or a casual bike ride, exerting about 50% of max effort. Yes, you will lose some muscle but the loss will be at a rate that is easy to replace. It is also good to vary the heart rate by 5-20% occasionally by walking on a slightly hilly surface. This works on your recovery heart rate.

- *High intensity/ long duration* is only recommended if you are participating in sports or activities that require this type. But be sure you understand the risk versus rewards.

CHAPTER *13*

Achieving Fitness Results

The priority for achieving Fitness Results is to build on a foundation of resistance weight training, proper nutrition and adequate rest. Once these three elements are second-nature, you can begin adding cardio to your health and fitness program.

When that time comes, I recommend two types of cardio training: *high-intensity/short duration* (HIIT, sometimes called *interval training*) and *low intensity/long duration* (such as a one hour walk). HIIT increases VO2 max — the ability of the cardiorespiratory system to transport oxygen to the tissues during a specified period of intense activity. It consists of exercising at an all-out pace for 30 seconds, then resting for 30 second to 2 minutes depending on the person's level of conditioning. Sprinting is an example of HIIT. HIIT is used by people who need to increase their aerobic capacity for performance. It mimics a strength-training session.

Low intensity/long duration cardio is based on RPE or *rate of perceived exhaustion,* a scale of 1-10 where 1 is effortless and 10 is the hardest thing you've ever done. To train correctly, you do a five minute warm-up, then an activity (walking, jogging, hiking, swimming, biking, rowing, etc.) with a starting pace of 5-6 RPE. At this pace you should be able to carry on a light conversation (3-5 words) and not be out of breath. Maintain this pace until you can no longer do so, usually 30-60 minutes. End with a 10-15 minute cool-down with static stretches. The lower the intensity, the longer the workout, and vice versa. Low intensity/long duration cardio training preserves muscle tissue by burning 50% muscle and 50% fat — generally the lowest ratio for any aerobic cardio activity.

I am not against doing cardio. I am against doing things that do not make sense. Deciding on the best way to achieve results for cardio training depends on your health and fitness goals. For those who want to lose weight, low intensity/long duration paired with resistance weight training is the safest and most efficient method. For those who don't need to lose much weight but need to change their body fat percentage, HIIT (such as running wind sprints) coupled with resistance weight training is recommended.

Those who love high intensity cardio training such as running marathons or long, intense bike rides can continue this activity, keeping in mind the twin risks of overtraining and injury. If that kind of cardio training is your passion, continue to do it. Just remember, you may be compromising your overall fitness goals. Keep your goals in mind and make good choices based on what you have learned from this book.

Why Resistance Weight Training is All You Need

You may have noticed that I have not included anything but resistance weight training exercises for major muscle groups: chest and back, legs (particularly quadriceps), and shoulders and arms. There is no separate core strengthening, yoga or Pilates, nor are there any exercises aimed at spot reducing target areas of the body. I have a reason for this. When you train the large muscles of the major muscle groups, the adjacent supportive muscle groups (abs, traps, neck, calves, forearms, etc.) will be simultaneously worked. Only competitive athletes would need to work other areas.

Your body has sets of muscle groups — right and left side, front and back, upper and lower — and it is very important that these groups stay in balance. When muscles are balanced, both sides are doing their part to hold bones in their proper positions and make your body work as it was designed to. For example, when viewed from behind, your shoulders will be at the same height. If you have an old muscle injury from past athletics causing limited range of motion or pain on the injury side, resistance weight training will strengthen weak muscles at the injury site. This will produce improved range of motion and will restore muscle balance. Now the supporting muscle groups no longer have to compensate for muscle imbalance and your body shape and posture will improve. You'll stand up straighter and move more easily.

Exercises aimed at spot reducing areas of the body not only don't work, they bring the risk of injury. What may be appropriate for someone competing in a physique contest or training for a particular sport does not support the goal of overall health and fitness. Spot reducing exercises can actually make body appearance worse. If you've been doing sit ups to work your abs and help get rid of belly fat, all you will accomplish is to push the belly fat layer out further and create a blocky or distended midsection.

Focusing intently on one muscle group causes stress on the associated joints and tendons, increasing your risk of injury. For example, your calves get a workout every time you take a step or pedal a bike which means they have adapted to that level of stress. To increase the stress, you would have to work them harder with lots of sets, reps and weight. This in turn puts unwanted stress on your feet, ankles, knees, hips and back. If the stress results in injury, you will have to take a break from training and rehab the injured area. During the break you will lose some of your Fitness Results and be worse off than if you hadn't started the spot training effort.

About Sports Performance and Functional Training

Sports performance and functional training are specialized types of fitness training. Their purpose is to increase speed, agility and reaction time needed for peak performance in a designated sport or physical activity. The training regime often consists of exercises and movements used in the sport or activity. Sports performance training has become popular with parents whose children are serious about athletics and for adults who are engaging in competitive sports.

Sports performance and functional training each has its place, but neither is a good substitute for basic resistance weight training. Here's why: imagine your body is a large ship. Small rowboats, each with four rowers aboard, are attached to the ship in order to move it forward. Sports performance and functional training teaches the rowers to move together with precision and exert maximum strength while avoiding injury. Compared to a ship whose rowers who haven't had this training, the ship will move more smoothly and quickly through the water.

But now imagine that each rowboat has eight rowers instead of four. This means each rowboat can apply twice as much strength to the task of moving the ship. And since strength (*i.e.* power) is necessary for speed, the four rowboats with eight rowers will be able to move the ship faster.

Resistance weight training is like adding extra rowers to each rowboat. Resistance weight training builds muscle mass, meaning more muscle fibers are available to work. As we learned in the sections of this book on muscle soreness and tips for a good workout, resistance weight training also teaches muscle fibers to work together, creating *muscle memory*. Over time, as you perform resistance weight training exercises with proper form, your muscle fibers will learn to work together throughout the entire range of motion. This produces strength, coordination and muscle tone — the basis for power, speed and reaction time.

If you lay down a solid foundation with resistance weight training, you can later add sports performance or functional training and achieve even greater fitness results than with sports performance or functional training alone.

Closing Thoughts on Achieving Fitness Results

Throughout this book I have emphasized what really works when it comes to achieving Fitness Results. I know this both from personal experience and from training clients of all ages and all stages of health and physical fitness. As you train, remember what you have learned and make good choices.

For most people, *it is neither too hard or nor time-consuming to achieve health and fitness goals.* Just 30 minutes three times a week — a mere hour and a half weekly — of resistance weight training will make a huge impact on your life. By following the principles and techniques in this book, 95% of people can get into the best shape of their lives, regardless of age. For years my clients have been astounded by how little time they spend working out, yet how great they feel and how much better their overall health and fitness is. Some clients find that by working with me, they spent much less time working out while still achieving far greater results than ever before.

Paying attention to your daily diet can make a big difference in losing weight and gaining muscle. Follow the guidelines and tips offered in this book and you can achieve and maintain your weight loss goals. Finally, *get adequate rest* at night and do not let your fitness and nutrition programs create stress in your life. Make a lifetime commitment to health and fitness and your body and mind will reward you. You can't stop time, but a good health and fitness program will slow the effects of time. It is the closest thing we have to the fountain of youth!

Be wary of celebrity-endorsed fad programs or pills, liquids or equipment that promise results without work. These are scams without a proven basis. Be aware that when you first begin your health and fitness program many people will support you. But strangely, after you make positive changes, some people will turn on you. They will begin making negative comments aimed at undermining your success. Ignore them. Don't let them deter you from your health and fitness path.

And *don't turn on yourself.* If you experience a break in your health and fitness routine because of vacation or injury or illness, don't give up.

Learn the signals that it is time to re-start your health and fitness program. If you find that you are tired and have no energy, or your old injury is painful again, or your weight goes up, remember that it is never as difficult to re-start as it was to begin initially. Get back to your health and fitness program and you'll soon get back to where you want to be.

More Stories of Clients Who Achieved Fitness Results

I don't dread Mondays because I love to start my work week. Don't get me wrong — I love my days off as much as you do. But what is satisfying for me about Monday through Thursday is helping my clients meet their health and fitness goals. Just as I used to challenge myself to meet fitness goals, now I challenge my clients. For myself, I work to maintain good health and keep the right balance of work and play. My challenges, which used to be personal, are now to help my clients — who include all ages from children to seniors and all fitness goals from health and wellness to professional athleticism — to meet their goals. I am proud to have guided so many clients through the years. Here are a few of many stories of clients who have achieved Fitness Results.

The ER physician. Dr. Grant is an emergency room physician and my longest continuous client. He was with me the first day I opened Fitness Results in 1994 and continues to train 2-3 days a week. A lot of marriages don't last that long!

Dr. Grant works at a local hospital and by now, after all his years of training, he could figure out how to work out on his own. But one of the advantages of having a personal trainer is that you don't have to think about your workouts. I do that for him. He trusts my training and experience and has been able to maintain good health. Recently we were talking about how long we've been training together, and he said working out with me is the best thing he could have done. In his words:

I am 70 years old. I feel younger than that because I can still do activities I enjoy. I firmly believe that my 20+ years with Lance at Fitness Results has played a major role in keeping me as "young" as I am today.

Dr. Grant – 70 years young!

The child. Josh started training with me when he was 11 years old. He weighed 258 lbs. and had over 50% body fat. He worked out 3 days a week and by his 14th birthday he weighed 160 lbs. and had 13.2% body fat — the healthiest range for his age.

At age 19 Josh's parents stopped paying for his training, but since he realized the value, he continued to train one day a week.

The top photo is Josh at age 20, weighing 175 lbs. still 13.2% body fat. That was lower than we wanted, so we gradually raised it to 17%.

The bottom photo is Josh today. He is 29 years old, still at 17% body fat, and is in great shape. He is gaining strength (he can bench press 255 lbs.) while staying fit and healthy.

The mom. A 29 year old woman came to me after the birth of her third child. She was having a hard time getting back into her pre-pregnancy shape. In three months she lost 30 lbs. and several inches, and went from 27% body fat to 15% body fat.

The Mom: 29 years old

3 month comparison

	Beginning training	After 3 months	Change
Weight	145 lbs.	115 lbs.	↓30 lbs.
Waist	31"	25"	↓6"
Hips	37.5"	35"	↓2.5"

The Seniors. A husband and wife in their 60s who were both overweight and starting to have health issues began training with small goals based on past success. They thought if they could lose around 20 lbs. each, they would be satisfied. After their assessments, I recommended goals that were much more aggressive than they thought possible. By applying what they were taught in my program, Patrick lost 74 lbs. and Nancy lost 58 lbs.

They both cut body fat from obese range to normal. Between them, they trimmed 20 inches from their waistlines and are now wearing the same size clothes as when they were in high school.

Patrick: 62 years old, 6'0'

15-month comparison

	Beginning training	After 15 months	Change
Weight	278 lbs.	206 lbs.	↓72 lbs.
Body fat percentage	35.8%	26.8%	↓8%
Fat lbs.	99.5 lbs.	55.5 lbs.	↓44 lbs.
Chest	51"	43"	↓8"
Waist	50.5"	39"	↓11.5"
Hips	49"	40.5"	↓8.5"
Upper leg	28.5"	23"	↓5.5"
Middle leg	25.5"	21.5"	↓4"
Arm	15.5"	13.5"	↓2"

Nancy: 63 years old, 5'6"

15-month comparison

	Beginning training	After 15 months	Change
Weight	195 lbs.	138.5 lbs.	↓56.6 lbs.
Body fat percentage	43.1%	31.7%	↓11.4%
Fat lbs.	84 lbs.	44 lbs.	↓40 lbs.
Chest	40.5"	33"	↓7.5"
Waist	41"	30"	↓11"
Hips	47.5"	38"	↓9.5"
Upper leg	27"	21"	↓6"
Middle leg	22.5"	18"	↓4.75"
Arm	13"	9.5"	↓3.5"

Left: Patrick and Nancy before training. **Right:** after 15 months.

Patrick and Nancy training together doing
shoulder cleans with dumbbells.

The Physically Fit Man. Gary, a 49-year-old client who had been working out every day, wanted to make even more gains. In three months he gained 12 lbs. of muscle and dropped from 17% body fat to 15%. He set a goal to bench press 315 lbs. before his 55th birthday. At 53 he achieved 265 lbs. and one year later, at 54, he reached his goal of 315 lbs. By his 55th birthday he was able to bench press 335 lbs.

Fundamental Fitness by Gary

Almost all of us strive or fantasize about "getting in shape" on a fairly regular basis. However, the daily pursuits of relationships, family, career and recreation all take their toll on our healthy ambitions. Not that being fit and healthy isn't important; it's just that it can be very difficult to make it a high priority in the general scheme of things.

My individual fitness journey started in earnest in late 2006. Working as a general manager for a large aerospace company and attempting to juggle the rest of my life was getting the best of me. Without going into all the details, I ended up checking into alcohol rehab at a pathetic 5'10" and 155 lbs. Besides my drinking problem I had acute pancreatitis and was near anorexic.

At this point I knew if I didn't fix the problem I wouldn't be around much longer. I wanted to be better, and do better. So I made a personal commitment to my sobriety. I also committed to get healthy and "in shape". This meant a great dedication to exercise, nutrition and healthy recreation.

Since I've been a very athletic person all my life, I decided I would start with weight training and running. I joined a local fitness gym and dove right in. I was training 4-5 days a week. With the help of a nutritionist from Kaiser Permanente, my nutrition also improved. I read and listened to everything I could about fitness and tried a lot of it.

After about a year and a half I had gained about 20 lbs. of muscle and my strength and endurance were greatly improved. My general health was much better and I really felt good. However, I was on the dreaded plateau. I amped up my workouts to 6 days a week for about two hours per session, but still no further improvement. I was getting discouraged but wouldn't dare give up.

At the time my secretary was training at a facility in Upland, California and I wanted to get her a gift certificate there as a Christmas gift. I went in, bought the certificate and started to talk with Lance McCullough, the owner of Fitness Results. He mentioned that it looked like I was into weight training. I said yes, but that I was currently completely stalled. He offered to perform an assessment for me at a convenient time in the future. I was somewhat wary but did schedule an appointment with Lance.

During the assessment several weeks later he weighed and measured me and checked my body fat. But mainly we chatted about what I had been doing and what kinds of goals I had. Lance quickly said that I was most likely overtraining for the type of muscle growth I was attempting. That is, I was lifting too often, with too many reps, and not enough weight. In order to progress I would need to lift less often, but with heavier weights and on a progressive regimen. Given Lance's world records and significant accomplishments in fitness and weight lifting, I decided to sign up with him to train me.

Lance put me on a structured regimen of fundamental weight training exercises. Nothing fancy, just heavy weights with strict form, 3-4 times a week, hitting a different body part each day of the week. After about three months I was definitely noticing the difference. I had gained about 8 lbs. of muscle and my bench press had increased by 25 lbs., to 250 lbs. In addition, my body fat had dropped from 18% down to 12%.

Lance and I began developing some rather lofty goals for the future which included, most notably, doing a 315 lb. bench press by my 55th birthday – about a year and half away. That would be six full 45 lb. plates on an Olympic bar. We worked hard in the gym and he also helped me focus my nutrition to support the goals. The other trainers and clients at

Fitness Results started tracking my progress and offering encouragement and support. I pledged to take the whole staff and all the clients to lunch when I made the 315 lb. goal.

One morning about 6 months before my 55th birthday, Lance and I were training chest and I had just confidently accomplished a 305 lb. bench press. We both looked at each other and knew that would be the day. Lance loaded another 10 lbs. on the bar and with my training partners chanting *just do it* – I did!

So the celebration luncheon at a local Italian restaurant the next week with all the Fitness Results staff and my training partners was sweet indeed. I knew without a doubt they all deserved the credit as much as I did.

Unfortunately, the next year I had to move to the East Coast and could no longer train at Fitness Results. I have maintained my training using the structure and knowledge Lance taught me. I stick with the fundamentals and I still lift heavy. I also do recreational type fitness endeavors like bicycling, rock climbing and golfing.

Most weeks someone in the gym asks me how old I am. That's usually followed by, "dude . . .you're in great shape for an old guy". I totally enjoy it because it means it's all still working for me.

Thanks again to Lance McCullough and Fitness Results!

* * *

In this section I have given you just a small sample of the vast success stories from my years as a personal trainer – and soon, I will be adding you to the list!

Beast and Beauty: A Winning Combination

This is the story of a short journey I had recently with Arnita Champion – a fitting last name, as she is now a professional figure competitor. Her story illustrates elements and conformation points for every chapter of the 30-Minute Body. (If you're not sure – in this story, I am the Beast and Arnita is the Beauty.)

Recall that I work with local colleges to offer their students internships in my gym. Many of my interns come from Mount San Antonio College, which is one of the best personal training programs in this area. Arnita works at Mt. SAC in the Career and Transfer Services Department as job developer. Arnita visited the gym a few times to talk, take photos of the interns working, and interview them after they begin employment at Fitness Results.

One day I learned from one of my interns who became a trainer that Arnita is a figure competitor, which I had not known before. (Figure competition is a class of physique-exhibition events for women.) A few weeks later during a visit to the gym, Arnita asked a question about training for her shoulders, which she felt were too narrow for competition. I had her stand facing me in a relaxed position so I could observe her hands. Exactly as I suspected, her palms were facing inward and knuckles facing out in front.

If your muscles are balanced and your posture correct, when you stand in a relaxed position, the palms of your hands will be facing your trunk. What Arnita's posture told me is that she had a muscular imbalance – her chest muscles were stronger than her back muscles. She had not been training her rear delts or back muscles correctly, so her stronger chest muscles were pulling her shoulders forward, producing the narrow look.

I asked Arnita if she was working her rear deltoids and back and she assured me that she was. Because I had limited time to help her that day, I gave her a stretching exercise to do on the foam roller. She implemented the rolling technique and the next time we spoke, she was happy with the results and noticed that her shoulders looked broader.

Arnita is 52 years old, a very nice person with a positive attitude and high energy. She posted to her social media account, highlighting me and Fitness Results for helping her. We became social media friends and started following each other.

A few weeks later, she competed in a National Physique Committee (NPC) national figure contest and came in fourth place. (NPC is the largest amateur bodybuilding organization in the United States.) At the level she competed in, everyone's goal is to win and thereby earn a pro card. Then you can compete at the very top of the sport, against the very best, in a professional competition.

But on her social media site, Arnita expressed disappointment with her fourth place finish. I sent her a message saying, "You should be very proud of your accomplishment of fourth place! Take it as an inspiration to move up next time. Please let me know if you need any help for your next competition."

That was on Saturday. The very next Monday Arnita called me asking for help. For her, this was a huge leap of faith. I am a world champion weight lifter, not a champion competitor in a physique contest. I am not as lean as I once was and sadly, at 5'10" and 290 lbs., I no longer have the shape I had when I was 35 years old and won my last competition. Knowing how many women are afraid of looking too manly, I was impressed that Arnita asked for my help.

We found a time to meet on Monday at Fitness Results. She shared her desire to compete at the next national pro qualifier event, to be held in just six weeks. I asked her for the specific areas where she most needed improvement. The judges had told her she needed more of a V shape with more lats. She mentioned that her calves were small and not well defined, and that overall she needed more muscle and definition.

Arnita and her coach had done a fine job to this point. Arnita worked hard and had dedication as well as great genetics for physique competition. I felt confident I could help her if she followed my Fitness Results Training System.

I recalled our previous conversation about her narrow shoulders. I knew her training was not balanced and after asking a few more questions, I knew she was over training. If she used a properly-designed program and trained with correct form, I knew she would blossom into a champion. She had a lot of pent-up potential but was not allowing her body to achieve because of over training, under resting, and lack of proper nutrition. Arnita took her leap of faith because I explained everything the entire training plan – what she was going to do, and why.

The first change was her diet. I set up a specific nutrition plan and made arrangements for a resting metabolic test. This would allow control of her weight and body fat by controlling her diet. Next, I had her drop all cardio except for jumping on her rebounder for 20 minutes two or three times a week – but only for health purposes, not to further her bodybuilding goals. She questioned me on this, and I explained that cardiovascular conditioning sacrifices muscle development. Since our goal was to build muscle, it wouldn't be logical to do cardio.

Next I told her to stop the ab-specific work she was used to. By way of explanation, I asked her why she wanted to continue ab work, even though her midsection was too thick. She could not come up with any answer except that she thought that's what you're supposed to do. I reminded her that when you work a muscle, it is stimulated and therefore gets bigger, so logically she should discontinue ab work until the week before the competition. To replace the ab work, I gave her breathing exercises to rebalance the core muscles and work them inward instead of outward as she had been doing.

I also taught her how to train the rear deltoids properly. She thought she had been training correctly, but in fact had not been training them at all. I taught her how to train her latissimus dorsi muscles correctly. She had been doing a lot of pulldowns and pull ups, but working the wrong muscles – exactly as I describe in the section on muscle balance.

Because I was extremely busy at the time, I had no room in my schedule to take on an additional client – especially one that would require a lot of time. And I wasn't sure if Arnita was willing to make the final investment required to accomplish her goals. So I proposed she train using the Fitness Results Training System, a blend of personal and small-group training. Here's how it works:

For each training session, the client logs in to her own personalized workout session, displayed as a table. The instructions lay out the weight and reps for the first warmup set and how long to rest before the next set. It sets a goal for the first working set based on the last time the exercise was performed. It provides a challenge to better the last workout. It assigns the next set based on the accomplishments of the previous set. Every day provides a unique workout, fully pre-pared and personalized. No workout is exactly the same as the one before because it always takes into account the results of the previous workout, what will be done today, and the goal for the future.

This system may sound too good to be true, but I assure you, it is real and working better than you can imagine. It is based on my lifetime of experience as a champion weightlifter and personal trainer with over 100,000 sessions of training clients. It is designed for people who cannot come to the Fitness Results gym, but want to use my training methods.

For motivation, I suggested that Arnita used the Fitness Results Training System and post her results on social media. Realizing the truth of the saying *Insanity is doing the same thing over and over again and expecting different results,* Arnita realized something needed to change.

And change she got! When I sent her first workout, she called me with a lot of questions, including *Is that all for this muscle group in the workout?* She had so many questions, she thought I had forgotten to send her the complete workout. I reassured her it was a very well thought out program and doing it correctly would produce the results she needed to win.

The next day when she came in for the resting metabolic test, we put together her detailed nutrition plan. Unlike the plans put forward by many contest coaches, the plan is based on the latest research and technology. I've heard some bizarre statements, such as *eat sweet potatoes but not brown rice* or *add a tablespoon of peanut butter* – weird, random advice. I've also heard contest coaches prescribe specific food and portions for every meal, which only a certified dietician can do.

For Arnita, I provided guidelines based on the content of the nutrition section of 30-Minute Body, with the exception of giving her a caloric budget to work within. We retested the following week and with feedback from the scale, made some adjustments. This was necessary because the first resting metabolic test was done just a few days after her last competition when her metabolic rate was greatly reduced from a very unhealthy program. After getting her on a properly designed nutrition program, weight training program, with proper rest and eliminating the destructive cardio training, within one week she almost doubled her metabolic rate.

Arnita was starting to feel and see changes. I received fewer calls with questions and she gained confidence day by day. Because Arnita was posting her workouts on social media, I could see short video clips and call her to suggest adjustments to form and range of motion. I told her how her trainer coach should spot her correctly by not helping her, but letting her work to total failure, and not giving her additional forced reps. Most of the corrections took hold quickly, though I did have her return to the gym one more time for hands-on training on squats and back exercises. Except for that, Arnita used the Fitness Results Training System remotely, with me providing her daily workout, and she sending me the number of reps she got on certain sets.

All was going smoothly until about two weeks before the competition. She wanted to begin ab-specific exercises in addition to the breathing exercises. Her waistline was 1.5" smaller already, so I told her to wait until a few days before the competition. At seven days away, I gave her a few exercises: just two sets and just a few reps, to light exertion. This was done for conditioning so she could pose without cramping.

Arnita's waist was 1.5" smaller and her latissimus dorsi muscles were greatly improved. I had her work her calves every day except for two, and in six weeks they were also greatly improved. Her overall muscular size, balance and conditioning were so much improved that she went from fourth place in her group to winning both her class and the all-over competition, and gained her coveted pro card!

All the techniques that transformed Arnita into a pro figure champion are explained in 30 Minute Body. Nothing special was added for her unique circumstance except for frequency and intensity. Just like Arnita, if you learn and use the information in 30 Minute Body, you will be able to achieve your health and fitness goals whether you are a child, a Baby Boomer, a stay-at-home mom, a business owner, professional football player or figure champion.

Arnita is not only a pro figure champion, she is also a very successful online personal trainer and social media star who has tens of thousands of followers. Her situation demonstrates that there are times when everyone, even professionals, can use the help of other professionals. Arnita had been working with a well-respected figure competitor coach, and they were following industry trends for training, nutrition and rest. Arnita achieved some results, but as she learned, just because everyone else is doing something one way, it doesn't mean it is the best or safest way.

This is a key to my success: I have never followed the crowd or done what's popular. Instead, I do the right thing based on scientific knowledge, experience and common sense.

Thank you, Arnita, for putting your faith in my expertise and my Fitness Results Training System and for showcasing my system on social media. Congratulations Arnita Champion pro figure competitor!

Arnita Tells Her Story

Change is good, but only when you know that the change you are embarking on is better than good. (That's what I think.) But what happens when you are not sure that the change you are making is better? That's where faith, trust, and the Fitness Results Training System come into play!

I was at a place in my fitness journey where I had the foundation to be competitive in the fitness arena. But I was tired of being competitive – I wanted to be PRO. In order to go from 3rd and 4th place, I needed to make a change.

I sought information from Lance McCullough. He saw the potential for me to obtain my pro card, but I had to stop doing what I was doing completely! Of course, this was foreign to me because I was used to a certain workout regimen. If I trusted the Fitness Results Training System, would it work for me in five short weeks?

Well, I had nothing to lose but my pro card! For the first week, anxiety, doubt and stress stared me in the face, especially when Lance told me to stop doing sit ups and cardio. Then joy came on the morning of the second week when I saw my waist had shrunk by 1¼ inch and my calves had grown.

Using the Fitness Results Training System, my meal plan/eating regimen was changed to enhance my desired muscle gain, and my workout was uniquely charted for no one but me. The increase in weights and reps, the decrease in weights and reps, the time in between sets, the correct form – you name it, it was covered. My workouts were calculated like science, I didn't have to guess what area to work on, or how much weight, or how many reps. It was precisely created just for me.

Because I trusted the Fitness Results Training System, I went from being competitive to being an IFBB (International Federation of Body Building) Pro Figure Competitor. The System changed my life and gave me a new title for life — IFBB PRO.

Could any other system do this? I don't think so. But I do know one thing for sure – I'm not going to try any of them.

It's hard to believe that the woman in these photographs is 52 years old. Yes, I know you're never supposed to reveal a lady's age, but this is almost unbelievable. On the left (light green bikini) is Arnita's fourth place physique - pretty amazing at this level of competition. On the right (patterned bikini) is her winning professional physique. Look closely with a trained eye and you'll see substantial differences in Arnita's overall musculature, body symmetry, and femininity.

This is a photo of Arnita and me. When she asked if I could help with her narrow shoulders, I gave her a copy of the Fitness Results Training Book which she then asked me to sign. Later she posted the photo on her social media site. I was the first person to endorse her as a professional figure competitor, so she sent me this photo as a reminder after she won her competition and pro card.

30 MINUTE BODY

Week 4

08/15/2016	Day 1	chest & Bicep		8/16/2016	Day 2	Quads		8/17/2016	Day 3	Back & Triceps		8/18/2016	Day 4	Shoulders & Arms 1 min rest every thing
Week 6 Bench Press 90%			Client	Date	Week 1 (Max Lbs)		Client	date	Week 2 Low Row		Client		Shoulder Cleans	
Warm Up			Actual		Squat		Actual		Warm Up		Actual		Warm Up	
Current Max	121			Current Max	135			Current Max	125			DB Press Max	35	1 rep
Set	Reps			Set	Weight	4 Reps	Reps	Set	Lbs	4 reps		Set	Lbs	Reps
1	40	6		Set 1	45	10	10	1	65	6		1	15	20
2	80	1		Set 2	70	10	10	2	95	3		2	15	20
3	100	1		Set 3	90	10	3	3	105	3		3	15	20
	120	0		Set 4	110	6 - 10	4	4	130	max		4	15	20

Chest Fly / Working Set

Set	Lbs	Reps		Set 5	135	4+	10	After 4th set				Rear Delt Fly		
1	120	max		Final Max	160	14+	145/8	If on set 4 you achieve Less than 3 sets				Set	Lbs	Reps
2	100	max				4	4	105	max			1	12	20
3	85	max		If on Set 6 you achieved 4+ reps				75	max			2	12	20
				Set 7		max	2	If on set 4 you achieve only 3, 4 reps				3	12	20

Chest Fly

Set	Reps			Set 7	130	max	15	1	105	max		side laterals		
1	35	15		Set 8	130	7		2	75	max		Set	Lbs	Reps
2	35	15		Set 9	130	max	1	After 4th set				1	12	20
3	35	15		Set 10	130	max	7	New max	136	max 4		2	12	20

Bicep Curls (A) alt db

6-10 rep Max	30 Lbs	4reps		Set 11	0	max	2					3	12	20
set	lbs	reps	Actual	Set 12	0	max	3			4 rep max				

Bicep Curls (B) DB

1	12.5	6	6		Leg Ext		Actual		High Row			Warm Up		
2	20	1		Set	Weight	Reps	Reps	Current Max	140			Current Max	25	4 reps
3	25	1		Set 1	165	10 - 15	15	Set	Lbs	Reps		Set	Lbs	Reps
4	30	1		Set 2	165	10 - 15	15	1	125	max		1	5	20
5	35	1		Set 3	160	10 - 15	15	2	105	max		2	10	20

If on Set 5 you achieved 10+ reps								3	85	max		3	20	20
5	40	max		calf standing								4	25	20

Warm Up — Lat Pull Down — Tricep (B) on back overhead — New Max 30 | 4

Arnita fourth week workout schedule (two weeks before competition)

Arnita fifth week workout schedule (one week before competition)

These are screen shots of Arnita's workout schedule for the fourth and fifth weeks (two weeks and one week before her competition). It shows the Personal Training Guide that is a part of the Fitness Results Training System. As you can see, each workout schedule is unique and designed for continuing improvements.

Notice that the warmup and working sets are laid out for Arnita. On max days, she inputs her max in the green box and the system automatically updates the rest of the workout with suggested reps or maximum reps. As Arnita trains, the system learns her training strengths and makes more specific rep suggestions. (The right-hand column shows the actual number of reps Arnita completed.) The system tracks Arnita's progress in every workout, then sets her new workout goals, enabling her to mentally prepare to better her previous performance.

To update workout goals, the system depended on Arnita's feedback following each workout. Because her competition date was coming, Arnita was very motivated and never forgot to provide feedback after each workout session.

You don't have to be as motivated as Arnita for the Fitness Results Training System to work for you. Should you forget to provide feedback, you will be contacted to see why and be given suggestions for staying on track and motivated. For more information about the Fitness Results Training System and the soon-to-be-released Fitness Results Training App, visit www.fitnessresultstrainingsystem.com.

CHAPTER 14

My Life Journey, or How I Developed My Training Philosophy

Throughout my life, I've always had a lot of energy and loved challenges. As early as elementary school, I remember wanting to run home instead of riding in the car with my brother and sisters when my mom came to pick us up. We only lived a mile or so from school, so on the days Mom would let me run, I would try to beat the car home. I'm not saying this was a smart thing to do — after all, they were in a car — but I still had to try.

As a high school freshman I played football. After hearing the stories of Hell Week, I was nervous, especially since I am the older brother and didn't have anyone to tell me what to expect. We started football practice and for weeks, I kept waiting for Hell Week to start. Finally I asked and was told that it had already happened, that it was the first week of practice. I was sorely disappointed; Hell Week was never much of a challenge for me.

Football is what got me into weight lifting. Part of football practice was to work out in the school gym. I had never lifted weights before so had no frame of reference for what was reasonable to do. My first day in the gym, a couple of my teammates did a bench press of 135 lbs. (the bar and one 45 lb. weight on each side). I was naturally muscular and on the bigger side, so I thought, *If they can do it, so can I* even though I had never done a bench press and hadn't warmed up. Of course, I failed. Turns out the guys both had older brothers they had been working out with, so they started already ahead of me.

I didn't like the feeling of failure, so for my birthday, I asked for a weight set. It was made of plastic with sand for weight and had a bench. It came with a workout book of basic exercises. Before long I could do everything in the book at the max of 110 lbs. I asked my dad for more weights and soon was doing many of the exercises with 200 lbs. When I returned to football practice my sophomore year and had access to even more weights, I realized that weight lifting was my true passion.

In football practice I excelled at weight lifting, but realized that the training itself was not effective. The coaches tolerated bad form and less-than-full range of motion so the football players could claim they could lift more weight. Afraid that I was not getting full results, I saved my money and joined a gym as soon as I turned 15. At the time, Southern California was the mecca of body building and weight lifting and several top weight lifters and body builders trained at my gym. They noticed my strength and began mentoring me, helping me learn the right techniques for effective lifting. Now I was hooked. I was at the gym seven days a week, making changes to improve my fitness results.

One of my accomplishments during high school that I am very proud of is attaining the rank of Eagle Scout in Boy Scouts. I had finished my Eagle Scout project just before I started working as a box boy at Alpha Beta. Thank goodness my project was done, because between working and weight lifting, I had very little extra time. I gave up sports, but was able to finish the rest of my Eagle Scout requirements before I was 18. My parents deserve the credit for encouraging and supporting me early on to achieve what I had started.

During my senior year in high school, I was given the opportunity to enroll in the meat cutting program — a possible career in a good-paying job. My store manager explained that I would need to start the program the next week. When I reminded him that I was still in high school, he said I could either make it happen or pass up the opportunity. I saw my school counselor, explained the opportunity, and discovered that I only needed to pass a social studies class and I'd have enough credits to graduate. I talked to the social studies teacher who said that if I completed my homework, I would pass the class and graduate. I did so and became a journeyman meat cutter.

My new job came with health benefits, so I began searching for a doctor who would help me maximize my fitness results through nutrition. All the many doctors I talked to knew nothing about nutrition to build muscle, and instead recommended steroid treatments (which were legal at the time). Not wanting to do that, I continued searching and eventually found a doctor of osteopathy who treated me almost like an intern in his office. He taught me about nutrition, body dynamics and digestion, and this became the foundation of my fitness program and training philosophy. I learned the complexities of nutrition and body dynamics, especially how everything is connected and in balance. For the next seven years, my life was working as a meat cutter, working out twice a day, and continuing to learn and advance my fitness program and fitness results.

Then things changed. A position called "meat clerk" was established which put me and many other meat cutters out of work. I tried construction for a while, but my passion was still weight lifting. The gym where I trained needed a manager, and the owner asked me if I would do it. I agreed, with the understanding that the job wouldn't interfere with my training. During this time, personal training was growing in popularity as a profession. Since I was already informally helping many people at the gym, I looked into what it would take to become a certified personal trainer. In 1989 I earned my certification from the Aerobics and Fitness Association of America (AFAA) and quickly built up a good clientele.

My personal training business grew rapidly. I was now at a different gym and the owner offered me a 20% interest if I would manage the gym. I saw this as an opportunity not only for me, but for my clients, as I would have control over how well the gym was running, so I agreed. Sometime later the owner was forced to close the gym for financial reasons but gave me his blessing to try to salvage the situation with the bank. I was newly married, so this was not a decision to make by myself. My wife Susie and I approached the bank and agreed on terms to buy the gym's equipment. Next we scrambled to find a suitable location, deciding on San Dimas since that is where we had recently bought a home. We found a location, obtained a business permit from the city, and in March 1994 Susie and I were in business as Fitness Results.

It was an exciting and terrifying time: newly-married, just bought a fixer-upper house, a new business and no regular paycheck. And it all worked out. The building was an industrial warehouse space with no air conditioning except in the cardio room. We moved the equipment out of the gym that was closing and into our facility. We began tenant improvements, moving the equipment from here to there as carpet was laid, lighting and ceiling fans were installed, mirrors, front counter and display cases were put in place. We stayed there for three years, building the business as a membership gym with personal training services.

The disadvantage of membership gym is the operating hours – 7 days a week and extended hours. In March 1997, we took two steps: we moved from warehouse space to professional/retail and changed from a membership to a personal training gym. I also refurbished the equipment by disassembling, sandblasting to remove paint, repainting and reassembling. It turned out so well that everyone thought the equipment was brand new. The new gym was a great success by referral. My clients — 125 to 135 personal training appointments a week — were achieving such great fitness results that word spread. I reached the point where I couldn't fit in any new clients, so decided to bring in other certified personal trainers to expand the gym's capacity.

While Fitness Results was growing in its second location, I was asked by a client if I would do a powerlifting meet with him. I had stopped competing years earlier and was reluctant to make the commitment. But he had done some research and showed me that the Amateur Athletic Union (AAU) was serious about having the highest standards of competition — the same as Olympic lifting. So I agreed to participate in the meet – the 1997 North American Powerlifting Championship.

That's my workout buddy Scotty giving me a lift off. If Scotty had not asked me to compete with him, I would never have accomplished what I did. Thank you, Scotty for the support and motivation!

At the time I weighed about 280 lbs. which would have put me and my client in the same weight class. He asked if I would move to a different class, so I decided to drop to the 242 lb. class. Once the decision was made, I was completely committed. Now every day I had a very stringent program of diet, training and rest. A few weeks before the competition, my client had a medical procedure and couldn't compete. Because I had trained for the meet and lost the necessary amount of weight, I went ahead with the competition. I won my class, even though it is extremely hard to keep up your strength while losing weight. And I did this while working full time.

The next year the same client wanted to compete in the 1998 North American Powerlifting Championship and again asked if I would do the meet with him. I agreed, but not in the 242 lb. weight class. At the time I was at around 260–265 lbs. and I felt good at that weight. We began training again, and just like the previous year, a few weeks prior to the competition my client backed out. I competed and won in what turned out to be the last qualifying competition for the 1998 United States Bench Press Championship. The AAU asked if I would enter the U.S. Bench Press Championship because they wanted their best lifters to compete and the competition was in Southern California. I agreed and the training continued. I competed and won, which qualified me for the 1998 World Bench Press Championship. While training I was trying to gain some weight but was only able to gain a few pounds. By competition day I was 268 lbs. and 14% body fat, lighter and leaner than I wanted to be. But it all worked out. I not only won the 1998 World Bench Press Championship, I achieved a new World Record!

And that was enough competition for me. When training at that level, injury prevention is always a challenge. I had more than two years without any major problems while training at the highest possible level of accomplishment with a very complex program and no room for error or deviation from the schedule. It was stressful but gratifying. I had pushed myself to the maximum level of fitness results and was satisfied.

With two years of training for competitions out of the way, Fitness Results continued to grow and help even more clients. More personal trainers on staff meant that we once again outgrew our location. We found a mixed-use industrial space in Upland being sold as a condo. Susie and I bought it and built it out exactly to my specifications. Everything was new, from the carpet and fixtures to the equipment. Every piece of equipment was picked for a purpose. I even went to Albuquerque, New Mexico to visit an equipment manufacturer.

My plan was to continue with my personal training clients in San Dimas and hire a manager for Upland. When at the last minute the manager candidate backed out, I found myself needing to spend more and more time at the Upland facility. I was handling clients at two locations, doing my best to provide 100% satisfactory services, and moving those who were willing to other staff trainers.

Upland continued to grow, while San Dimas stagnated. When the Great Recession of 2008 hit, my landlord in San Dimas raised my rent (a great surprise, since other landlords were adjusting rents downward). I closed the San Dimas location in October 2010. Some of my San Dimas clients made the move to Upland; others did not. My only disappointment in opening the Upland gym is being forced to make changes to my existing clients. I sold most of the San Dimas equipment to one of my corporate wellness accounts. It is a relief to be in just one location.

The most recent change for the gym is our expansion into the adjacent condo. We purchased the unit in 2012, doubling our square footage to 6000, and again built it out to my specifications. The expansion is more open and very modular, with the original space serving personal training clients and the expansion serving fitness groups and sports teams with TRX training, Kangoo Jump and hip hop dance classes, bouldering, speed and agility training and Olympic lifting. With more space I was able to offer internships for personal training students from Mount San Antonio

Left: personal training side of gym. Right: group fitness side. Two gyms in one!

College. This has provided a stream of good trainers, enabling me to select the best to work at Fitness Results. The rest go on to other gyms equipped with practical knowledge from their internship to augment their studies.

The future of Fitness Results is bright. We are always working on ways to reach out and help more people get on the right path to their Fitness Results. The original Fitness Results Training Book (inspired by the Fitness Results Training System) led to the 30-Minute Body, the Fitness Results Training System app, and the Fitness Results Training Academy. For the first two decades of Fitness Results, I have been constrained to only being able to change the lives of people who live in proximity to my brick-and-mortar gym. The new Fitness Results Training System allows me to spread health and fitness to everyone.

The reason I have been so successful is that my training system really works. When a new client begins to realize their health and fitness goals, it changes everything for them. They have more energy and a more positive attitude. They are happier and look and feel better. Everyone around them notices and wants the same change. It becomes infectious as friends and family also begin to be healthy and fit.

My dream is that the Fitness Results Training System will have the same effect for a much broader audience. The 30-Minute Body introduces the foundation of the art, science, principles and behavior embodied in the Fitness Results Training System. The Fitness Results Training System app provides a step-by-step program for every aspect of your workout: all phases of the exercises (warmup, max weight and rest); setting goals; tracking advancements; never doing exactly the same workout. The Fitness Results Training System is completely unique and unlike anything else you've read about or heard about because it is based on my lifelong experiences as World Record Bench Press Champion and over 100,000 sessions of personal training delivered!

Thank you for your interest in my story. My purpose in telling it is because I want you to know where your information is coming from. There is a lot of information in the world — both reliable and unreliable — so please be sure yours is coming from a qualified source.

Best wishes on your fitness journey. I look forward to hearing your success stories. Please send them to <u>lance@fitnessresults.com</u>. I am excited to hear them and post them on the Fitness Results web site.

The McCullough family – Susie, Lance and four-legged kids Max and Amber.

Sample Meal Plans

1200-Calorie Diet

Day 1

Breakfast

- 3 egg white omelet with 1 cup of spinach, ¼ cup onion, topped with 3 tbsp. salsa and ¼ of an avocado
- 1 slice of whole wheat dry toast
- 1 small apple

Lunch

- Salad: 5 cups of romaine lettuce, 1 cup chopped strawberry, 0.5 oz. walnuts with 2 tbsp. raspberry vinegar dressing
- 3 oz. skinless chicken breast
- 2 hard-boiled egg whites

Dinner

- 3 oz. filet mignon, ¾ cup sweet potato, 1 cup broccoli, and 1 cup asparagus.

Total calories for the day: 1,195 (Protein 30%; Carbs 40%; Fat 30%)
Protein 86 g; Carbs 121g; Fat 40g; Fiber 32g

Day 2

Breakfast

- 4 egg whites scrambled with 2 tbsp. salsa on top

- 1 cup oatmeal cooked with ½ cup blueberries and 1/8 cup almonds

Lunch

- Sandwich: 2 slices whole wheat bread; 3 oz. chicken breast (butterflied and broiled with salt and pepper in advance); 2 tsp. spicy brown mustard (or to taste); romaine lettuce; ¼ avocado

Snack

- ½ cup fat free cottage cheese, 1 orange and 1/8 cup almonds.

Dinner

- Salad: 2 cups arugula, 2 cups spinach, 3 oz. salmon, and ½ cup strawberries mixed with ½ lemon juice and ½ tbsp. extra virgin olive oil

Total calories for the day: 1,195 (Protein 30%; Carbs 40%; Fat 30%) Protein 90 g; Carbs 119 g; Fat 39 g; Fiber 23.8 g

Day 3

Breakfast

- 1 serving nonfat Greek yogurt with ¼ cup strawberries and ¼ cup blueberries, and 1 slice whole wheat toast.

Lunch

- Subway 6" turkey sandwich with light mayonnaise and veggies

Snack

- 8 almonds and Subway apple slices

Dinner

- Claim Jumper Ahi Spinach salad

Total calories for the day: 1,195 (Protein 30%; Carbs 40%; Fat 30%) Protein 83 g; Carbs 115 g; Fat 39 g; Fiber 15.4 g

For additional meal plans and recipes, go to www.fitnessresults.com

1500-Calorie Diet

Day 1

Breakfast

- Shake: blend 1 avocado, 2 cups arugula, 2 cups spinach, 1 oz. beet juice Lakewood, 6g chia seeds, 7g flax seed, 4 egg whites (or substitute protein powder)

Lunch

- 2 cups spinach sautéed with ½ cup white beans, topped with 6 oz. salmon, 10 green olives and 2 tbsp. salsa
- ½ sweet potato
- 1 small apple

Dinner

- Sauté 6 oz. chicken breast with 1 tbsp. coconut oil, 2 cups broccoli. Serve with ½ cup brown rice

Total calories for the day: 1,50395 (Protein 29%; Carbs 42%; Fat 29%) Protein 108 g; Carbs 157 g; Fat 48 g; Fiber 35.6 g,

Day 2

Breakfast

- 1 McDonald's Egg White Delight McMuffin, 2 McDonald's apple slices

Lunch

- Carl's Jr. Original Grilled Chicken Salad with low fat balsamic vinaigrette dressing

Snack

- Carl's Jr. Low Carb Charbroiled Chicken Club -- no bacon, cheese or mayonnaise

Dinner

- McDonald's Premium Southwest Salad with grilled chicken, low fat balsamic vinaigrette -- no tortilla strips, no cheese
- 2 McDonald's apple slices

Total calories for the day: 1,442 (Protein 30%; Carbs 40%; Fat 30%) Protein 104 g; Carbs 143 g; Fat 50 g; Fiber 20 g

Day 3

Breakfast

- Cinnamon apple oatmeal: ⅓ cup oats, ⅔ cup skim milk, ½ cup chopped apple, 2 tbsp. chopped walnuts

Snack

- 1 cup carrot sticks with 3 tbsp. hummus

Lunch

- Veggie quesadilla: 1 whole-wheat tortilla stuffed with ⅓ cup low-fat shredded Cheddar cheese, ¼ cup black beans, ¼ cup each sliced peppers and mushrooms sautéed in 1 tsp. olive oil. Serve with ¼ avocado, sliced

Dinner

- Garlic-Basil Shrimp & Zucchini Pasta: 1 cup whole-wheat pasta noodles, 3 oz. frozen precooked and shelled shrimp, thawed, 1 cup chopped zucchini, 2 tablespoons chopped fresh basil, 2 garlic cloves minced, 1 tablespoon olive oil.

Total calories for the day: 1,460 (Protein 30%; Carbs 40%; Fat 30%) Protein 113 g; C 150 g; Fat 50 g

For additional meal plans and recipes, go to www.fitnessresults.com

Exercise Descriptions

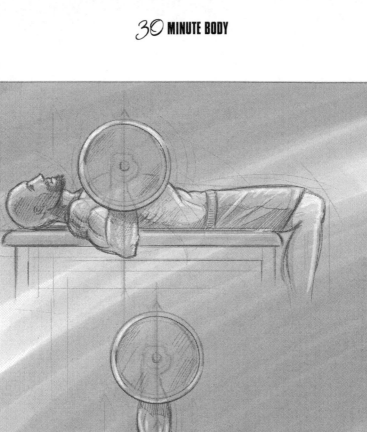

Bench Press

Bench Press

Target muscle: chest

Starting Position

1. Lie flat on back on the bench, gluts (buttocks) flat, abdominals stable to achieve neutral spine, feet resting flat on floor.
2. Position body so the bar is over the upper portion of the chest.
3. Position hands on the bar to be equidistant from the center of the bar with thumbs in line with the outside of the shoulders. (This is called a *neutral grip*. Other possible grips are *close grip* and *wide grip*.)
4. Lift the bar from the supports, raise straight up and hold over the upper portion of the chest.

Downward Movement

1. Lower the bar to the chest, aiming for a point just above the nipple line. Keep forearms perpendicular to the floor and in line with the elbows. (If you are using a close grip, aim for a spot lower on the chest; if a wide grip, aim for a higher position on the chest.)
2. Maintain control during the entire downward movement.

Upward Movement

1. To complete one rep, extend the arms straight up to full extension while maintaining control, abdominal stabilization and neutral spine.

Ending Movement

1. From max extension, move the bar backwards toward the cradle.
2. Lower the bar into the cradle.
3. Sit up and step away from the bench.

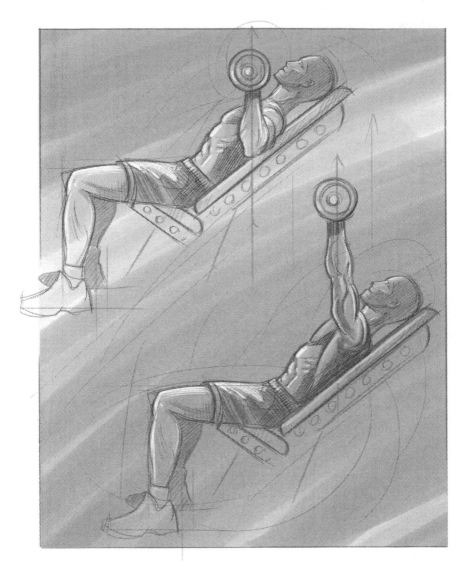

Incline Bench Press with Dumbbells

Incline Bench Press with Dumbbells

Target muscle: chest

Starting Position

1. Position bench at 30-45 degree incline.
2. Sit on bench with dumbbells resting on knees, palms facing each other.
3. Raise knees to push dumbbells up and back while simultaneously lowering body to incline position.
4. Raise dumbbells to armpit level with hands positioned at shoulder width, palms facing out and feet flat on ground.

Upward Movement

1. Push the dumbbells to full extension while keeping the dumbbells in line with the elbows, wrists rigid and forearms perpendicular to the floor. (The hands may move toward each other slightly in an upside down "V" shape.)
2. Maintain control, abdominal stabilization and neutral spine.

Downward Movement

1. Lower the dumbbells to full contraction while keeping the dumbbells in line with the elbows, wrists rigid and forearms perpendicular to the floor.
2. Maintain control, abdominal stabilization and neutral spine.

Ending Movement

1. From max contraction, lower the dumbbells while simultaneously raising the knees to absorb the impact of the weights.
2. Stand and step away from the bench.

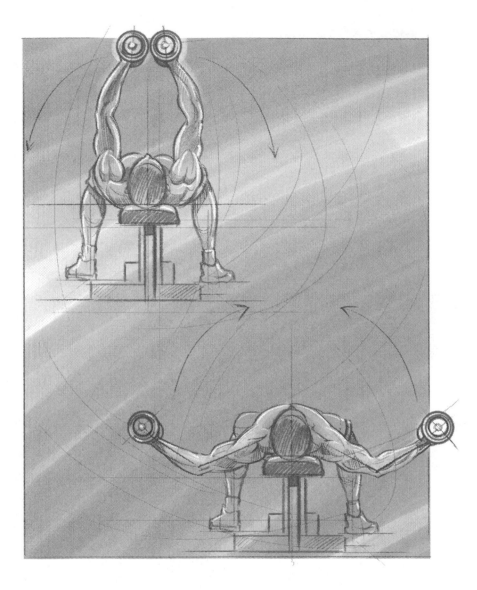

Lying Chest Fly with Dumbbells

Lying Chest Fly with Dumbbells

Target muscle: chest
This is not a strength exercise; it is a dynamic stretch.

Starting Position

1. Sit on bench with dumbbells resting on thighs.
2. Lower upper body to lie flat on back, buttocks flat, abdominals stable to achieve neutral spine, feet resting flat on floor.
3. Raise dumbbells to shoulder level directly over chest in full extension, palms facing in.

Downward Movement

1. While keeping the wrists straight and elbows slightly bent in line with the chest, lower the dumbbells in a wide arc, bringing the arms parallel to chest in a light stretch.
2. Maintain control, abdominal stabilization and neutral spine.

Upward Movement

1. Raise the dumbbells upward in a wide arc to full extension as if hugging a very large tree trunk with the arms.
2. Keep the wrists straight and the elbows in a slightly bent position.
3. Maintain control, abdominal stabilization and neutral spine.

Ending Movement

1. Lower the dumbbells to thighs.
2. Sit up.
3. Stand and step away from the bench.

Lat Pulldown with High Pulley Bar

Lat Pulldown with High Pulley Bar

Target muscle: back and lats
Primary muscles used: latissimus dorsi and pectoral major

Starting position

1. Adjust seat so feet touch the ground
2. Adjust thigh pad so it is snug on top of thigh
3. Grip the bar so hands on the bar are equidistant from the center, thumbs are in line with outside of shoulders and facing out.
4. Sit down, positioning thighs under thigh pad, feet flat on the ground, back straight and abdominals stable.

Downward movement

1. Keeping back straight, pull elbow down to full contraction, hands following elbows.
2. Maintain control, abdominal stabilization and neutral spine.

Upward movement

1. While maintaining control, extend up to maximum extension.

Ending Movement

1. Rise slowly while gripping the bar.
2. When fully standing and the weight is resting, release the bar and step away from the machine.

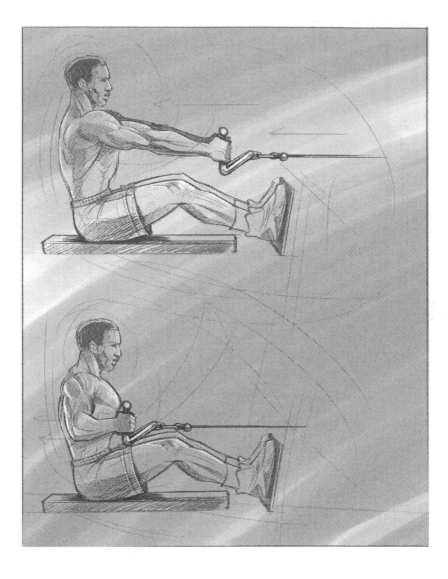

Low Row Using Low Pulley

Low Row Using Low Pulley

Target muscle: midback
Primary muscles used: latissimus dorsi and deltoids

Starting Position

1. Sit upright on the bench with feet on foot pads, knees slightly bent and abdominals stable to create neutral spine.
2. Lean forward to grip the pulley handles with palms facing each other.
3. Return to upright position, raising the weight stack.

Contracting (Pulling) Movement

1. Using a smooth, even movement, pull elbows back to full contraction while keeping them close to the body and just above waist level. Hands follow the elbows.
2. Maintain control, abdominal stabilization and neutral spine.

Forward Movement

1. While maintaining control, extend arms to full extension and return handles to the starting, contracting position.
2. Maintain control, abdominal stabilization and neutral spine.

Ending Movement

1. Lean forward slowly while continuing to grip handles until they come to rest.
2. Release handles, rise and step away from the machine.

Incline Bench Rhomboid Row with Dumbbells

Incline Bench Rhomboid Row with Dumbbells

Target muscle: rhomboid and upper back

Starting Position

1. Position bench at 30-45 degree incline.
2. While gripping dumbbells, sit on the bench with upper body bending forward until chest rests on pad.
3. Straighten back and neck so they are in line and stabilize abdominals.
4. Lower arms down the side of the bench with elbows slightly bent to be in line with the chest.

Upward Movement

1. Keeping back straight, pull elbows back to full contraction while keeping them out away from the body and at chest level. Hands follow the elbows.
2. Maintain control, abdominal stabilization and neutral spine.

Downward Movement

1. Lower the dumbbells in a smooth, continuous movement to full lower position.
2. Maintain control, keep back and neck in line and abdominals stable.

Seated Shoulder Press with Dumbbells

Seated Shoulder Press with Dumbbells

Target muscle: shoulders

Starting position

1. Sit on bench with dumbbells resting on knees, palms facing each other.
2. Raise knees to push dumbbells up and back to shoulder level with hands positioned at shoulder width, palms facing out, feet flat on ground, and abdominals stable to maintain neutral spine.

Upward movement

1. Push the dumbbells up to full extension over the shoulders while keeping the dumbbells in line with the elbows, wrists rigid and forearms perpendicular to the floor.
2. Maintain control, abdominal stabilization and neutral spine.

Downward movement

1. Lower the dumbbells to the shoulders in full contraction while keeping the dumbbells in line with shoulders, wrists rigid and forearms perpendicular to the floor.
2. Maintain control, abdominal stabilization and neutral spine.

Ending Movement

1. From max contraction, lower the dumbbells while simultaneously raising the knees to absorb the impact of the weights.
2. Stand and step away from the bench.

Shoulder Press Clean with Dumbbells

Shoulder Press Clean with Dumbbells

Target muscle: shoulders (rotator cuff muscles)

Starting Position

1. Grasp the dumbbells.
2. Stand straight with knees slightly bent, feet shoulder width apart, abdominals stable to maintain neutral spine, and arms fully extended toward the floor.

Upward Movement

1. Lift the dumbbells by bending arms at the elbows and continue in a smooth motion to full extension over head. Do not stop the movement at shoulders.

Downward Movement

1. In a continual smooth movement, lower dumbbells back to the starting position without stopping at shoulders.
2. Maintain control, abdominal stabilization and neutral spine.

Incline Bench Deltoid Fly with Dumbbells

Incline Bench Deltoid Fly with Dumbbells

Target muscle: rear deltoids

Starting Position

1. Position bench at 30-45 degree incline.
2. While gripping dumbbells, sit on the bench with upper body bending forward until chest rests on pad.
3. Straighten back and neck so they are in line and stabilize abdominals.
4. Lower arms down the side of the bench with elbows slightly bent to be in line with the chest.

Upward Movement

1. Raise the dumbbells in a wide arc with elbows following forearms, until the hands are slightly above shoulder level in a light stretch. At the apex of the arc, elbows will be slightly in front of shoulders, but at no greater angle than 45 degrees.
2. Maintain control, keep back and neck straight and in line; and abdominals stable.

Downward Movement

1. Lower the dumbbells in a smooth, continuous movement to full lower position
2. Do not allow any movement to occur at the elbow joints, only the shoulders.
3. Maintain control, keep back and neck in line and abdominals stable.

Standing Side Laterals with Dumbbells

Standing Side Laterals with Dumbbells

Target muscle: outer shoulder (posterior deltoid)

Starting Position

1. Grasp the dumbbells.
2. Stand straight with knees slightly bent, feet shoulder width apart, abdominals stable to maintain neutral spine.
3. Position arms at side of body with elbows fully extended toward the floor and palms facing inward (*i.e.,* toward the body).

Upward Movement

1. In a slow, controlled movement, raise arms simultaneously away from the torso to shoulder height, forming a "T".
2. Keep elbows extended and wrists rigid.
3. With the arms slightly bent and using a slow, controlled movement, raise arms simultaneously by pulling the elbows away from the torso to shoulder height. Keep forearms in same plane as elbows and wrists straight.
4. Do not shrug the shoulders
5. Maintain control, keep back and neck straight, knees slightly bent and abdominals stable

Downward Movement

1. Using a slow, controlled movement, lower the dumbbells to the torso in full contraction. Do not bounce the dumbbells on the thigh at the bottom of the movement.
2. Maintain control, keep back and neck straight, knees slightly bent and abdominals stable.

Biceps Standing Curl with Bar

Biceps Standing Curl with Bar

Target muscle: biceps
Primary muscles used: biceps brachii

Starting Position

1. Stand with knees slightly bent, back straight and abdominals stable.
2. With palms facing up, grasp the barbell keeping hands a shoulder width apart.

Upward Movement

1. Lift the barbell from the cradle by simultaneously bending the elbow of each arm to full contraction, keeping the wrist straight and stable.
2. Maintain control, keep back straight and abdominals stable.

Downward Movement

1. Using a smooth and continuous motion, lower the lower barbell until arm is 99% extended.
2. Maintain control, keep back straight and abdominals stable.

Ending Movement

1. Place the barbell in the cradle.

Triceps Push Down with Straight Bar and High Pulley

Triceps Push Down with Straight Bar and High Pulley

Target muscle: triceps

Starting Position

1. Stand facing pulley with back straight and shoulders back and down, feet shoulder width apart, elbows at side and knees slightly bent.
2. Grasp bar positioning hands to be shoulder width apart with palms down.
3. Keep elbows close to torso, slightly in front of shoulders

Downward Movement

1. Pull down on bar and straighten elbows to full extension
2. Keep elbows at side of torso as if pinned there.
3. Keep shoulders down and back, torso erect and abdominals stable.

Upward Movement

1. Using a controlled and continuous movement, raise bar to full contraction
2. Keep shoulders down and back with elbows against torso, slightly in front of shoulders.
3. Maintain control, keep torso erect and abdominals stable.

Free Squat with Bar

Free Squat with Bar

Target muscles: quadriceps, hamstrings, gluts

Starting Position

1. Position bar on rack about shoulder height.
2. Stand at the center of the bar, facing it, with feet shoulder width apart and body close to the bar.
3. Grip the bar with both hands equidistant from the center of the bar slightly wider than shoulder width.
4. Bend at the waist and knees to lower your head under the bar.
5. Remove bar from cradles and bring to rest on back and trapezoid muscles.
6. Stabilize abdominals to create neutral spine, straighten legs, and take 1-2 steps back to allow room for movement.

Downward Movement

1. While maintaining neutral spine and stable abdominals, lower torso by bending knees, shins slightly forward. Allow hips to bend and back to move slightly forward to maintain balance. Keep knees pointed in same direction as feet.
2. Keeping feet flat on floor, descend until knees are fully bent (*i.e.,* the hip joint and knee joint are parallel).
3. Maintain control during the entire downward movement.

Upward Movement

1. While maintaining neutral spine and stable abdominals, raise torso until legs are straight. Keep feet flat on floor.
2. Maintain control during the entire upward movement.

Ending Movement and Dismount

1. While maintaining neutral spine and stable abdominals, take 1-2 small steps toward rack.
2. Bend knees to lower bar back to cradles while maintaining stable abdominals and neutral spine.

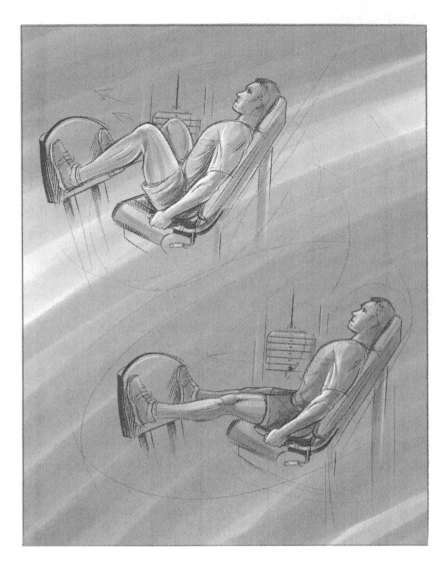

Leg Press

Leg Press

Target muscles: quadriceps, hamstrings, gluts

Starting Position

1. Sit on bench with back well supported by seat back and shoulders against shoulder pads.
2. Place feet near the middle of the plate at shoulder width.
3. Stabilize abdominals and keep back flat.

Pushing or Forward Movement

1. Keeping the weight evenly distributed between feet, extend legs straight out in a controlled, forceful motion.
2. Do not let toes lift up while pushing the weight.
3. Keep back flat with stable abdominals.

Downward or Backward Movement

1. With abdominals stable and using a controlled movement, contract legs by bending the knees until weight stack almost touches the base.

Ending Movement and Dismount

1. Gently let weights settle on weight stack.
2. Relax, remove feet and dismount.

Leg Extension

Leg Extension

Target muscle: quadriceps

Starting Position

1. Sit on bench with buttocks and back against pads. Align knees with pivot point of leg raise bar.
2. Position feet under the padding of the moving part of the machine. Knees should be bent at approximately a 90 degree angle.

Upward Movement

1. Using a smooth, controlled movement, straighten legs to full extension while maintaining stable abdominals and neutral spine.
2. Do not arch or move back forward. Do not rotate pelvis.

Downward Movement

1. Using a smooth, controlled movement, lower legs to starting position.
2. Maintain stable abdominals and neutral spine. Do not arch back or rotate pelvis.

Prone Leg Curl

Prone Leg Curl

Target muscle: hamstrings

Starting Position

1. Lie face down on bench. Adjust position so backs of ankles are under the padding of the moving part of the machine. Align knees with the pivot point of the leg curl bar.
2. Grasp handles of machine for support.

Upward Movement

1. Using a controlled, smooth motion, move feet toward buttocks by bending the knees. Do not use hips to assist or let back arch.
2. Maintain stable abdominals and keep head aligned with spine.

Downward Movement

1. Using a controlled, smooth movement, lower legs to straight position.

Shoulder External Rotation (dynamic stretch)

Shoulder External Rotation (dynamic stretch)

Target muscle: rear deltoids
Equipment needed: resistance band
Frequency: three sets of 20 reps, twice a week

Starting Position

1. Stand erect with both arms, including elbows, tight to torso. If desired, hold a magazine between arm and torso to help keep the arm and elbow in proper position.
2. Hold the resistance band taut in hands between both hands at waist level, forearms straight ahead at a 90 degree angle to torso and parallel to the floor.
3. Stabilize abdominals.

Movement (sideways)

1. While maintaining neutral spine and stable abdominals, move one hand away from body in full range of motion, keeping elbow tight to torso. (Full range of motion = the point just short of discomfort. If using a magazine, it should not fall from between arm and torso.)
2. Keep forearm at 90 degree angle to torso and parallel to the floor.
3. After reaching full range of motion, use a controlled and smooth movement to bring hand to starting position.
4. Repeat for second side.

Shoulder Rotator Cuff (dynamic stretch)

Shoulder Rotator Cuff (dynamic stretch)

Target muscle: rotator cuff
Frequency: three sets of 20 reps, twice a week

Starting Position

1. Stand erect with right arm straight and away from body at 45 degree angle to torso.
2. Point thumb down toward floor.
3. Stabilize abdominals to maintain neutral spine.

Movement (up and down)

1. While maintaining neutral spine and stable abdominals, bring right arm straight upwards in a controlled, smooth movement to full range of motion. (Full range of motion = the point just short of discomfort.)
2. Using a controlled, smooth movement, return to starting position.
3. Repeat for left side.

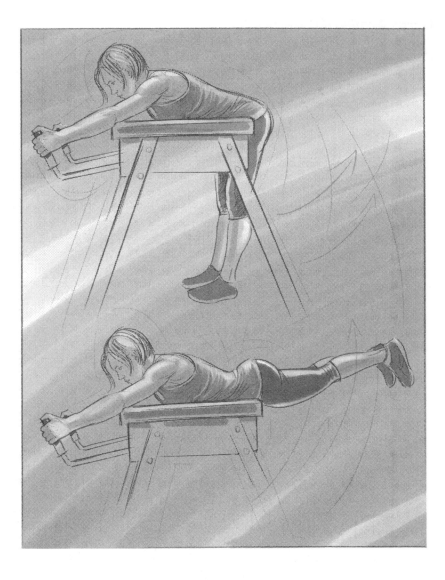

Low Back Reverse Hyper (dynamic stretch)

Low Back Reverse Hyper (dynamic stretch)

Target muscle: lower back and spine

Starting Position

1. Stand at end of machine and position left foot under padding of the moving part of the machine.
2. With right foot, step up and lie face down on bench. Grasp handles of machine for support.
3. Position right foot under padding of the moving part of the machine.
4. Stabilize abdominals.

Movement (up and down)

1. Using a controlled, smooth movement and keeping hips on bench, raise legs to full range of motion.
2. Maintain control and abdominal stability.
3. Using a controlled, smooth movement, return to starting position.

Nutrition Guidelines
& Journals

NUTRITION GUIDELINES: PROTEIN

SUGGESTED DAILY SERVINGS	WOMENS 3 SERVINGS					MEN 3-4 SERVINGS				
FOOD	PORTION	CALORIES	CARB	PROTEIN	FAT	PORTION	CALORIES	CARB	PROTEIN	FAT
Beef, ground extra lean, pan fried	3 oz.	225	0	21g	14g	6 oz.	434	0g	42g	2g
Beef, top sirloin, meat only, broiled	3 oz.	166	0	26g	6.1g	6 oz.	332	0g	52g	12.2g
Chicken breast, meat only, roasted	3/4 each	107	0	24g	3.1g	1 oz.	142	0g	48g	6.2g
Halibut, dry heat	3 oz.	119	0	23g	2.5g	6 oz.	238	0g	46g	5g
Pork loin, meat only, roasted	3 oz.	178	0	29g	8.2g	6 oz.	356	0g	58g	16.4g
Salmon, pink, dry heat	3 oz.	127	0	22g	3.8g	6 oz.	254	0g	44g	7.6g
Steak, beef tenderloin, lean only, broiled	3 oz.	179	0	24g	8.5g	6 oz.	358	0g	48g	17g
Swordfish, dry heat	3 oz.	132	0	22g	4.4g	6 oz.	264	0g	44g	8.8g
Tuna, canned in water	3 oz.	98	0	21g	8g	6 oz.	196	0g	42g	16g
Turkey breast, regular lunch meat	4 slices	124	3.2	3.2g	3.2g	5 oz.	155	3.2g	3.2g	3.2g
Large egg	1 each	78	0.6	6g	5g	1 each	78	6g	6g	5g
Egg white, raw	3 each	51	0	12g	0g	6 each	102	0g	24g	0g
Egg substitute, frozen, Egg Beaters	1/2 cup	60	2	12g	0g	1 cup	120	4g	24g	0g
Milk, skim, fat free	6 fl. oz.	65	9	6g	0.3g	12 fl. oz.	130	18g	12g	0.6g
Mozzarella cheese, part skim milk	1 oz.	49	1	7g	4.5g	2 oz.	98	2g	14g	9g
Cottage cheese, dry nonfat	1/2 cup	42	2	7g	0.5g	1 cup	84	4g	14g	1g

NUTRITION GUIDELINES: COMPLEX CARBOHYDRATES

SUGGESTED DAILY SERVINGS	WOMEN 2-3 SERVINGS					MEN 3-4 SERVINGS				
FOOD	PORTION	CALORIES	CARB	PROTEIN	FAT	PORTION	CALORIES	CARB	PROTEIN	FAT
Barley, cooked	1/4 cup	99	23g	2g	0.35g	1/2 cup	198	48g	4g	0.7g
Quinoa	1/4 cup	156.25	27.25g	6g	2.5g	1/2 cup	312.5	54.6g	12g	5g
Cream of wheat, prepared	1/2 cup	120	25g	3g	0g	1 cup	240	50g	6g	0g
Oatmeal, prepared	1/2 cup	79	13.5g	3g	1.6g	1 cup	158	27g	6g	3.2g
Sweet potato	1/2 cup	57	13.5g	1.05g	0.1g	1 cup	114	27g	2.1g	0.1g
Rice, brown, cooked	1/4 cup	54	11.25g	1g	0.25g	1/2 cup	108	22.5g	2.5g	0.9g
Rice, white, long grain, cooked	1/2 cup	108	22.5g	2.5g	0.9g	1 cup	216	45g	5g	1.8g
Spaghetti, cooked with salt	1/2 cup	110.5	21.5g	4g	0.65g	1 cup	221	43g	8g	1.3g
Spaghetti, whole wheat, cooked	1/2 cup	87.5	18.6g	3.75g	0.5g	1 cup	175	37.2g	7.5g	1g
Baked potato, with skin, medium	1/2 cup	161	37g	4g	0.2g	1 med	161	37g	4.3g	0.2g
Corn on the cob, boiled	1/4 cup	151.5	30.75g	4g	2g	1/2 cup	303	61.5g	8g	4g
Yam	1/2 cup	88.5	21g	1.15g	0.15g	1 cup	177	42g	2.3g	0.3g
Lentils, cooked	1/2 cup	115	20g	9g	0.4g	1 cup	230	40g	18g	0.8g
Pinto beans, cooked	1/2 cup	122.5	22.4g	7.7g	0.55g	1 cup	245	44.8g	15.4g	1.1g
Bread, multigrain, whole-grain, 7-grain	1 slice	65	12g	3g	0.2g	2 slices	130	24g	6g	0.4g
Bread, oat bran, regular	1 slice	71	12g	3g	1.3g	2 slices	142	24g	6g	2.6g

NUTRITION GUIDELINES: SIMPLE CARBOHYDRATES

SUGGESTED DAILY SERVINGS: Women 2-3; Men 2-4

FOOD	PORTION	CALORIES	CARB	PROTEIN	FAT
Apples, fresh with skin	1 each	81	21g	0g	0.5g
Bananas, fresh	1/2 each	55	14g	1g	0.3g
Blackberries, fresh	1/2 cup	37	9g	1g	0.3g
Blueberries, fresh	1/2 cup	41	10g	0g	0.3g
Cantaloupe, fresh wedge, 1/8 melon	6 oz.	37	9g	1g	0.5g
Grapefruit, fresh, pink or red	1 each	74	18g	2g	0.2g
Grapes, American type	30 each	48	12g	0g	0.3g
Melon, Honeydew, fresh	1 cup	62	16g	0g	0.2g
Nectarines, fresh	1 each	67	16g	1g	0.6g
Orange, fresh	1 each	65	16g	1g	0.3g
Pears, fresh	1 each	98	25g	1g	0.7g
Pineapple, fresh	1/2 cup	38	10g	0g	0.3g
Strawberries, fresh	9 each	33	8g	0g	0.5g
Watermelon, fresh, 1/16 melon wedge	6 oz.	55	12g	1g	0.7g

NUTRITION GUIDELINES: FIBERS AND MICRONUTRIENTS

SUGGESTED DAILY SERVINGS: Women 4 or more; Men 5 or more					
FOOD	PORTION OUNCE	CALORIES	CARB	PROTEIN	FAT
Asparagus, cooked	1/2 cup	22	4g	2g	0.3g
Broccoli, cooked	1/2 cup	22	4g	2g	0.3g
Carrots, fresh	1 each	31	7g	1g	0.1g
Cauliflower, fresh	1/2 cup	13	3g	1g	0.1g
Celery, fresh	1 each	6	1g	0g	0.1g
Cucumber, fresh, with peel	1/2 each	20	4g	1g	0.2g
Green beans, fresh, cooked	1/2 cup	22	5g	1g	0.2g
Lettuce, iceberg	1 cup	7	1g	1g	0.1g
Mushrooms, fresh	1/2 cup	8	1g	1g	0.1g
Onions, fresh	1/4 each	11	2g	0g	0.1g
Peppers, hot green chili, canned no seeds	1	15	4g	1g	0.1g
Peppers, sweet green, fresh	1 each	32	8g	1g	0.1g
Salad greens, mixed, fresh	1 each	32	8g	1g	0.2g
Spinach, cooked	1/2 cup	21	3g	3g	0.2g
Spinach, fresh	1 cup	7	1g	1g	0.1g
Sprouts, alfalfa, fresh	1 cup	10	1g	1g	0.2g
Tomatoes, fresh	1 each	26	6g	1g	0.1g
Zucchini, cooked, sliced	1/2 cup	14	4g	1g	0.1g
Salsa, regular	4 tbsp.	18	4g	0g	0.2g

NUTRITION GUIDELINES: FATS

SUGGESTED DAILY SERVINGS: Women 3; Men 3-4

FOOD	PORTION	CALORIES	CARB	PROTEIN	FAT
Peanut Butter, with salt	1 tbsp.	95	3g	4g	8.1g
Peanuts, dry roasted with salt	0.5 oz.	83	3g	4g	7.1g
Cashew, dry roasted with salt	0.5 oz.	82	5g	2g	6.6g
Almonds, regular	0.5 oz.	82	3g	3g	7.2g
Olive oil	1 tbsp.	40	0g	0g	4.5g
Avocados, fresh California, 1/4 avocado		77	3g	1g	7.6g

CARDIO RECOMMENDATIONS

FREQUENCY	DURATION	INTENSITY	TYPE

FREQUENCY	DURATION	INTENSITY	TYPE

FREQUENCY	DURATION	INTENSITY	TYPE

FREQUENCY	DURATION	INTENSITY	TYPE

Food Journal

Date _____ S M T W T F S   Daily Total Calories _____

BREAKFAST	LUNCH	DINNER	SNACK
Calories _____	Calories _____	Calories _____	Calories _____
Protein % _____	Protein % _____	Protein % _____	Protein % _____
Carbs % _____	Carbs % _____	Carbs % _____	Carbs % _____
Fat % _____	Fat % _____	Fat % _____	Fat % _____
Fiber gm _____	Fiber gm _____	Fiber gm _____	Fiber gm _____

Daily Nutrition Journal

Date _____	Date _____	Date _____	Date _____
Day _____	Day _____	Day _____	Day _____
Calories _____	Calories _____	Calories _____	Calories _____
Protein % _____	Protein % _____	Protein % _____	Protein % _____
Carbs % _____	Carbs % _____	Carbs % _____	Carbs % _____
Fat % _____	Fat % _____	Fat % _____	Fat % _____
Fiber gm _____	Fiber gm _____	Fiber gm _____	Fiber gm _____

Date _____	Date _____	Date _____	Date _____
Day _____	Day _____	Day _____	Day _____
Calories _____	Calories _____	Calories _____	Calories _____
Protein % _____	Protein % _____	Protein % _____	Protein % _____
Carbs % _____	Carbs % _____	Carbs % _____	Carbs % _____
Fat % _____	Fat % _____	Fat % _____	Fat % _____
Fiber gm _____	Fiber gm _____	Fiber gm _____	Fiber gm _____

To download a PDF of this page, go to www.fitnessresults.com

30 **MINUTE BODY**

Goal Tracking

Height _____   Date of Birth: _____   Age _____   Date _____

_____

_____

_____

_____

_____

_____

_____

_____

_____

_____

_____

_____

_____

_____

_____

Body Weight

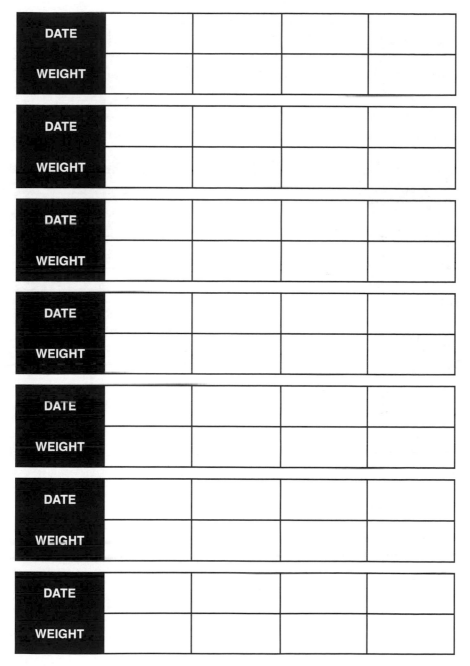

DATE				
WEIGHT				

DATE				
WEIGHT				

DATE				
WEIGHT				

DATE				
WEIGHT				

DATE				
WEIGHT				

DATE				
WEIGHT				

DATE				
WEIGHT				

To download a PDF of this page, go to www.fitnessresults.com

$3O$ MINUTE BODY

Fat %
(Total Fat in lbs & BME)

DATE				
FAT %				
BODY FAT				
BMI				

DATE				
FAT %				
BODY FAT				
BMI				

DATE				
FAT %				
BODY FAT				
BMI				

DATE				
FAT %				
BODY FAT				
BMI				

DATE				
FAT %				
BODY FAT				
BMI				

DATE				
FAT %				
BODY FAT				
BMI				

Measurements

DATE				
NECK				
CHEST				
WAIST				
HIPS				
UPPER LEG				
MIDDLE LEG				
KNEE				
CALF				
ARM				

DATE				
NECK				
CHEST				
WAIST				
HIPS				
UPPER LEG				
MIDDLE LEG				
KNEE				
CALF				
ARM				

DATE				
NECK				
CHEST				
WAIST				
HIPS				
UPPER LEG				
MIDDLE LEG				
KNEE				
CALF				
ARM				

To download a PDF of this page, go to www.fitnessresults.com

Carrying a big log around is one way to achieve fitness results; another way is to journal your workouts. Now you know how to make the right choice.

Strength Log: Chest and Shoulders

To download a PDF of this page, go to www.fitnessresults.com

Chest	Exercise	1 Rep Max at 100%	80-90% Max	High Rep Max at 50%
	Bench Press			
	DB Incline Press			
	Machine Press			
Shoulders	DB Shoulder Press			
	Machine Shoulder Press			
	DB Rear Delt Flies			
Shoulders	TRX Y Fly	N/A	N/A	

Strength Log: Arms

To download a PDF of this page, go to *www.fitnessresults.com*

Exercise	1 Rep Max at 100%	80-90% Max	High Rep Max at 50%
DB Tricep Extension			
Overhead Rope Extension			
TRX Tricep Extension	N/A	N/A	
EZ Bar Curls			
TRX Curls	N/A	N/A	
DB Curls			

Strength Log: Back

To download a PDF of this page, go to www.fitnessresults.com

Exercise	1 Rep Max at 100%	80-90% Max	High Rep Max at 50%
BA Pulldown			
Lat Pulldown			
Rhomboid Row			
Low Row			
Machine Row			
TRX Mid Row	N/A	N/A	
TRX Low Row	N/A	N/A	

Strength Log: Legs

To download a PDF of this page, go to www.fitnessresults.com

Exercise	1 Rep Max at 100%	80-90% Max	High Rep Max at 50%
Barbell Squat			
Hack Squat			
Perfect Squat			
Leg Press			
TRX Rip Squats	N/A	N/A	
TRX Squat	N/A	N/A	

Made in the USA
San Bernardino, CA
08 January 2019